edexcel

advancing learning, changing lives

BTEC National
Travel and Tourism

Study Guide

A PEARSON COMPANY

BTEC National Study Guide: Travel and Tourism

Published by:
Edexcel Limited
One90 High Holborn
London WC1V 7BH
www.edexcel.org.uk

Distributed by:
Pearson Education Limited
Edinburgh Gate
Harlow
Essex CM20 2JE

First published 2007
Third impression 2008

ISBN 978-1-84690-225-3

Project managed and typeset by Hart McLeod, Cambridge
Printed in Great Britain by Ashford Colour Press Ltd, Gosport, Hants.

Cover ©Atmotu Images/Alamy

The publisher's policy is to use paper manufactured from sustainable forests.

The Publishers and authors are grateful for the following for permission to reproduce text within copyright:
Page 44 Travel Trade Gazette; 45-6 Tourism Knowledge; 47 Express Newspapers; 48 BBC News Interactive; 49 Express Newspapers; 50 Opodo Ltd.; 51 Travel Trade Gazette; 53 Copyright Guardian News & Media Ltd 2005; 54 Adfero – www.adfero.co.uk; 58-9 Visit Britain; 63 The Scotsman Publications Ltd; 65-67 Visit Britain; 66 Copyright Guardian News & Media Ltd 2005; 68-70 Copyright Guardian News & Media Ltd 2005; 71 Visit Brighton; 72 Enjoy England; 73-4 Visit Britain; 79 Crystal Holidays; 79-80 First Choice Holidays & Flights; 93-4 First Choice Holidays & Flights; 102 Business Travel Direct; 103 Hogg Robinson Group; 106-10 Travel Weekly; 109-10 Travel Trade Gazette; 110-11 Travel Counsellors; 111-12 Travel Weekly; 149 Timesonline; NISyndication.

Every effort has been made to trace copyright holders and we apologise in advance for any unintentional omissions. We would be pleased to insert the appropriate acknowledgement in any subsequent edition of this publication.

Images
p.53 ©Craig Lovell/Corbis; p.55 ©John Conrad/Corbis; p.62 top ©Digital Vision/Getty, bottom ©James Leynse/Corbis; p.68 ©Dennis Stone/Rex Features; p.71 ©World Pictures/Alamy; p.73 ©Richard Klune/Corbis; p.74 ©Rex Butcher/Jon Arnold Images/Alamy p.86 ©Walter Lockwood/Corbis; p.87 ©Helene Rogers/Alamy; p.90 ©Image Source/Corbis; p.101 ©Image Source/Corbis; p.103 ©Jon Feingersh/zefa/Corbis; p.112 ©Jose Luis Pelaez,Inc.,/Blend Images/Corbis; p.125 ©Arco Images/Alamy

This material offers high quality support for the delivery of Edexcel qualifications.
This does not mean that it is essential to achieve any Edexcel qualification, nor does it mean that this is the only suitable

Contents

PREFACE

If you've already followed a BTEC First programme, you will know that this is an exciting way to study; if you are fresh from GCSEs you will find that from now on you will be in charge of your own learning. This guide has been written specially for you, to help get you started and then succeed on your BTEC National course.

The **Introduction** concentrates on making sure you have all the right facts about your course at your fingertips. Also, it guides you through the important skills you need to develop if you want to do well including:

■ managing your time

■ researching information

■ preparing a presentation.

Keep this by your side throughout your course and dip into it whenever you need to.

The **Activities** give you tasks to do on your own, in a small group or as a class. They will help you internalise your learning and then prepare for assessment by practising your skills and showing you how much you know. These activities are not for assessment.

The sample **Marked Assignments** show you what other students have done to gain Pass, Merit or Distinction. By seeing what past students have done, you should be able to improve your own grade.

Your BTEC National will cover six, twelve or eighteen units depending on whether you are doing an Award, Certificate or Diploma. In this guide the activities cover sections from Unit 1 – Investigating Travel and Tourism, Unit 3 – The UK as a Destination, Unit 6 – Preparing for Employment in the Travel and Tourism Industry and Unit 9 – Retail and Business Travel Operations. These units underpin your study of Travel and Tourism.

Because the guide covers only four units, it is essential that you do all the other work your tutors set you. You will have to research information in textbooks, in the library and on the Internet. You should have the opportunity to visit local organisations and welcome visiting speakers to your institution. This is a great way to find out more about your chosen vocational area – the type of jobs that are available and what the work is really like.

This Guide is a taster, an introduction to your BTEC National. Use it as such and make the most of the rich learning environment that your tutors will provide for you. Your BTEC National will give you an excellent base for further study, a broad understanding of travel and tourism and the knowledge you need to succeed in the world of work. Remember, thousands of students have achieved a BTEC National and are now studying for a degree, or at work building a successful career.

INTRODUCTION

SEVEN STEPS TO SUCCESS ON YOUR BTEC NATIONAL

You have received this guide because you have decided to do a BTEC National qualification. You may even have started your course. At this stage you should feel good about your decision. BTEC Nationals have many benefits – they are well-known and respected qualifications, they provide excellent preparation for future work or help you to get into university if that is your aim. If you are already at work, then gaining a BTEC National will increase your value to your employer and help to prepare you for promotion.

Despite all these benefits though, you may be rather apprehensive about your ability to cope. Or you may be wildly enthusiastic about the whole course! More probably, you are somewhere between the two – perhaps quietly confident most of the time but sometimes worried that you may get out of your depth as the course progresses. You may be certain you made the right choice or still have days when your decision worries you. You may understand exactly what the course entails and what you have to do – or still feel rather bewildered, given all the new stuff you have to get your head around.

Your tutors will use the induction sessions at the start of your course to explain the important information they want you to know. At the time, though, it can be difficult to remember everything. This is especially true if you have just left school and are now studying in a new environment, among a group of people you have only just met. It is often only later that you think of useful questions to ask. Sometimes, misunderstandings or difficulties may only surface weeks or months into a course – and may continue for some time unless they are quickly resolved.

This Student Guide has been written to help to minimise these difficulties, so that you get the most out of your BTEC National course from day one. You can read through it at your own pace. You can look back at it whenever you have a problem or query.

This Introduction concentrates on making sure you have all the right facts about your course at your fingertips. This includes a **Glossary** (on page 32) which explains the specialist terms you may hear or read – including words and phrases highlighted in bold type in this Introduction.

The Introduction also guides you through the important skills you need to develop if you want to do well – such as managing your time, researching information and preparing a presentation; as well as reminding you about the key skills you will need to do justice to your work, such as good written and verbal communications.

Make sure you have all the right facts

5

- Use the PlusPoint boxes in each section to help you to stay focused on the essentials.

- Use the Action Point boxes to check out things you need to know or do right now.

- Refer to the Glossary (on page 32) if you need to check the meaning of any of the specialist terms you may hear or read.

Remember, thousands of students have achieved BTEC National Diplomas and are now studying for a degree, or at work building a successful career. Many were nervous and unsure of themselves at the outset – and very few experienced absolutely no setbacks during the course. What they did have, though, was a belief in their own ability to do well if they concentrated on getting things right, one step at a time. This Introduction enables you to do exactly the same!

STEP ONE

UNDERSTAND YOUR COURSE AND HOW IT WORKS

What is a BTEC qualification and what does it involve? What will you be expected to do on the course? What can you do afterwards? How does this National differ from 'A' levels or a BTEC First qualification?

All these are common questions – but not all prospective students ask them! Did you? And, if so, did you really listen to the answers? And can you remember them now?

If you have already completed a BTEC First course then you may know some of the answers – although you may not appreciate some of the differences between that course and your new one.

Let's start by checking out the basics.

- All BTEC National qualifications are **vocational** or **work-related**. This doesn't mean that they give you all the skills that you need to do a job. It does mean that you gain the specific knowledge and understanding relevant to your chosen subject or area of work. This means that when you start in a job you will learn how to do the work more quickly and should progress further. If you are already employed, it means you become more valuable to your employer. You can choose to study a BTEC National in a wide range of vocational areas, such as Business, Health and Social Care, IT, Performing Arts and many others.

- There are three types of BTEC National qualification and each has a different number of units.

  - The BTEC National Award usually has 6 units and takes 360 **guided learning hours (GLH)** to complete. It is often offered as a part-time or short course but you may be one of the many students doing an Award alongside 'A' levels as a full-time course. An Award is equivalent to one 'A' level.

  - The BTEC National Certificate usually has 12 units and takes 720 GLH to complete. You may be able to study for the Certificate on a part-time or full-time course. It is equivalent to two 'A' levels.

6

– The BTEC National Diploma usually has 18 units and takes 1080 GLH to complete. It is normally offered as a two-year full-time course. It is equivalent to three 'A' levels.

These qualifications are often described as **nested**. This means that they fit inside each other (rather like Russian dolls!) because the same units are common to them all. This means that if you want to progress from one to another you can do so easily by simply completing more units.

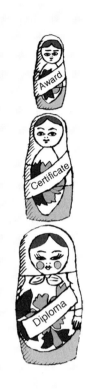

- Every BTEC National qualification has a set number of **core units**. These are the compulsory units every student must complete. The number of core units you will do on your course depends upon the vocational area you are studying.

- All BTEC National qualifications also have a range of **specialist units** from which you may be able to make a choice. These enable you to study particular areas in more depth.

- Some BTEC National qualifications have **specialist core units**. These are mandatory units you will have to complete if you want to follow a particular pathway in certain vocational areas. Engineering is an example of a qualification with the overarching title, Engineering, which has a set of core units that all students must complete. Then, depending on what type of engineering a student wants to follow, there are more specialist core units that must be studied.

- On all BTEC courses you are expected to be in charge of your own learning. If you have completed a BTEC First, you will already have been introduced to this idea, but you can expect the situation to be rather different now that you are working at BTEC National level. Students on a BTEC First course will be expected to need more guidance whilst they develop their skills and find their feet. In some cases, this might last quite some time. On a BTEC National course you will be expected to take more responsibility for yourself and your own learning, almost from the outset. You will quickly be expected to start thinking for yourself. This means planning what to do and carrying out a task without needing constant reminders. This doesn't mean that your tutor won't give you help and guidance when you need it. It does mean, though, that you need to be 'self-starting' and to be able to use your own initiative. You also need to be able to assess your own performance and make improvements when necessary. If you enjoy having the freedom to make your own decisions and work at your own pace then you will welcome this type of learning with open arms. However, there are dangers! If you are a procrastinator (look up this word if you don't know what it means!) then it's quite likely that you will quickly get in a muddle. In this case read Step 3 – Use your time wisely – very carefully indeed!

- The way you are assessed and graded on a BTEC course is different from an 'A' level course, although you will still obtain UCAS points, which you need if you want to go to university. You can read about this in the next section.

PLUSPOINTS

+ You can usually choose to study part-time or full-time for your BTEC National and do an Award, Certificate or Diploma and progress easily from one to the other.

+ You will study both core units and specialist units on your course.

+ When you have completed your BTEC course you can get a job (or **apprenticeship**), use your qualification to develop your career and/or continue your studies to degree level.

+ You are responsible for your own learning on a BTEC course. This prepares you for life at work or at university when you will be expected to be self-starting and to use your own initiative.

ACTION POINTS

✓ Check you know whether you are studying for an Award, Certificate or Diploma and find out the number of units you will be studying for your BTEC National qualification.

✓ Find out which are core and which are specialist units, and which specialist units are offered at your school or college.

✓ Check out the length of your course and when you will be studying each unit.

✓ Explore the Edexcel website al www.edexcel.org.uk. Your first task is to find what's available for your particular BTEC National qualification. Start by finding National qualifications, then look for your vocational area and check you are looking at the 2007 schemes. Then find the specification for your course. Don't print this out – it is far too long. You could, of course, save it if you want to refer to it regularly or you could just look through it for interest and then bookmark the pages relating to your qualification for future reference.

✓ Score yourself out of 5 (where 0 is awful and 5 is excellent) on each of the following to see how much improvement is needed for you to become responsible for your own learning!

Being punctual; organisational ability; tidiness; working accurately; finding and correcting own mistakes; solving problems; accepting responsibility; working with details; planning how to do a job; using own initiative; thinking up new ideas; meeting deadlines.

✓ Draw up your own action plan to improve any areas where you are weak. Talk this through at your next individual **tutorial**.

STEP TWO

UNDERSTAND HOW YOU ARE ASSESSED AND GRADED – AND USE THIS KNOWLEDGE TO YOUR ADVANTAGE!

If you already have a BTEC First qualification, you may think that you don't need to read this section because you assume that BTEC National is simply more of the same. Whilst there are some broad similarities, you will now be working at an entirely different level and the grades you get for your work could be absolutely crucial to your future plans.

Equally, if you have opted for BTEC National rather than 'A' level because you thought you would have less work (or writing) to do then you need to read this section very carefully. Indeed, if you chose your BTEC National because you thought it would guarantee you an easy life, you are likely to get quite a shock when reality hits home!

It is true that, unlike 'A' levels, there are no exams on a BTEC course. However, to do well you need to understand the importance of your assignments, how these are graded and how these convert into unit points and UCAS points. This is the focus of this section.

Your assignments

On a BTEC National course your learning is assessed by means of **assignments** set by your tutors and given to you to complete throughout your course.

■ Your tutors will use a variety of **assessment methods**, such as case studies, projects, presentations and shows to obtain evidence of your skills and knowledge to date. You may also be given work-based or **time-constrained** assignments – where your performance might be observed and assessed. It will depend very much on the vocational area you are studying (see also page 16).

- Important skills you will need to learn are how to research information (see page 25) and how to use your time effectively, particularly if you have to cope with several assignments at the same time (see page 12). You may also be expected to work co-operatively as a member of a team to complete some parts of your assignments – especially if you are doing a subject like Performing Arts – or to prepare a presentation (see page 26).

- All your assignments are based on **learning outcomes** set by Edexcel. These are listed for each unit in your course specification. You have to meet *all* the learning outcomes to pass the unit.

Your grades

On a BTEC National course, assignments that meet the learning outcomes are graded as Pass, Merit or Distinction.

- The difference between these grades has very little to do with how much you write! Edexcel sets out the **grading criteria** for the different grades in a **grading grid**. This identifies the **higher-level skills** you have to demonstrate to earn a higher grade. You can find out more about this, and read examples of good (and not so good) answers to assignments at Pass, Merit and Distinction level in the marked assignments section starting on page 114. You will also find out more about getting the best grade you can in Step 5 – Understand your assessment – on page 16.

- Your grades for all your assignments earn you **unit points**. The number of points you get for each unit is added together and your total score determines your final grade(s) for the qualification – Pass, Merit or Distinction. You get one final grade if you are taking a BTEC National Award, two if you are taking a BTEC National Certificate and three if you are taking a BTEC National Diploma.

- Your points and overall grade(s) also convert to **UCAS points** which you will need if you want to apply to study on a degree course. As an example, if you are studying a BTEC National Diploma, and achieve three final pass grades you will achieve 120 UCAS points. If you achieve three final distinction grades the number of UCAS points you have earned goes up to 360.

- It is important to note that you start earning both unit and UCAS points from the very first assignment you complete! This means that if you take a long time to settle into your course, or to start working productively, you could easily lose valuable points for quite some time. If you have your heart set on a particular university or degree course then this could limit your choices. Whichever way you look at it, it is silly to squander potentially good grades for an assignment, and their equivalent points, just because you didn't really understand what you had to do – which is why this guide has been written to help you!

■ If you take a little time to understand how **grade boundaries** work, you can see where you need to concentrate your efforts to get the best final grade possible. Let's give a simple example. Chris and Shaheeda both want to go to university and have worked hard on their BTEC National Diploma course. Chris ends with a total score of 226 unit points which converts to 280 UCAS points. Shaheeda ends with a total score of 228 unit points – just two points more – which converts to 320 UCAS points! This is because a score of between 204 and 227 unit points gives 280 UCAS points, whereas a score of 228 – 251 points gives 320 UCAS points. Shaheeda is pleased because this increases her chances of getting a place on the degree course she wants. Chris is annoyed. He says that if he had known, then he would have put more effort into his last assignment to get two points more.

■ It is always tempting to spend time on work you like doing, rather than work you don't – but this can be a mistake if you have already done the best you can at an assignment and it would already earn a very good grade. Instead you should now concentrate on improving an assignment which covers an area where you know you are weak, because this will boost your overall grade(s). You will learn more about this in Step 3 – Use your time wisely.

PLUSPOINTS

+ Your learning is assessed in a variety of ways, such as by assignments, projects and case studies. You will need to be able to research effectively, manage your own time and work well with other people to succeed.

+ You need to demonstrate specific knowledge and skills to achieve the learning outcomes set by Edexcel. You need to demonstrate you can meet all the learning outcomes to pass a unit.

+ Higher-level skills are required for higher grades. The grading criteria for Pass, Merit and Distinction are set out in a grading grid for the unit.

+ The assessment grades of Pass, Merit and Distinction convert to unit points. The total number of unit points you receive during the course determines your final overall grade(s) and the UCAS points you have earned.

+ Working effectively from the beginning maximises your chances of achieving a good qualification grade. Understanding grade boundaries enables you to get the best final grade(s) possible.

ACTION POINTS

✓ Find the learning outcomes for the units you are currently studying. Your tutor may have given you these already, or you can find them in the specification for your course that you already accessed at www.edexcel.org.uk.

✓ Look at the grading grid for the units and identify the way the evidence required changes to achieve the higher grades. Don't worry if there are some words that you do not understand – these are explained in more detail on page 32 of this guide.

✓ If you are still unsure how the unit points system works, ask your tutor to explain it to you.

✓ Check out the number of UCAS points you would need for any course or university in which you are interested.

✓ Keep a record of the unit points you earn throughout your course and check regularly how this is affecting your overall grade(s), based on the grade boundaries for your qualification. Your tutor will give you this information or you can check it yourself in the specification for your course on the Edexcel website.

USE YOUR TIME WISELY

Most students on a BTEC National course are trying to combine their course commitments with a number of others – such as a job (either full- or part-time) and family responsibilities. In addition, they still want time to meet with friends, enjoy a social life and keep up hobbies and interests that they have.

Starting the course doesn't mean that you have to hide away for months if you want to do well. It does mean that you have to use your time wisely if you want to do well, stay sane and keep a balance in your life.

You will only do this if you make time work for you, rather than against you, by taking control. This means that you decide what you are doing, when you are doing it and work purposefully; rather than simply reacting to problems or panicking madly because you've yet another deadline staring you in the face.

Use your time wisely

This becomes even more important as your course progresses because your workload is likely to increase, particularly towards the end of a term. In the early days you may be beautifully organised and able to cope easily. Then you may find you have several tasks to complete simultaneously as well as some research to start. Then you get two assignments in the same week from different tutors – as well as having a presentation to prepare. Then another assignment is scheduled for the following week – and so on. This is not because your tutors are being deliberately difficult. Indeed, most will try to schedule your assignments to avoid such clashes. The problem, of course, is that none of your tutors can assess your abilities until you have learned something – so if several units start and end at the same time it is highly likely that there will be some overlap between your assignments.

To cope when the going gets tough, without collapsing into an exhausted heap, you need to learn a few time-management skills.

- **Pinpoint where your time goes at the moment** Time is like money – it's usually difficult to work out where it all went! Work out how much time you currently spend at college, at work, at home and on social activities. Check, too, how much time you waste each week – and why this happens. Are you disorganised or do you easily get distracted? Then identify commitments that are vital and those that are optional, so that you know where you can find time if you need to.

- **Plan when and where to work** It is realistic to expect to do quite a lot of work for your course in your own time. It is also better to work regularly, and in relatively short bursts, than to work just once or twice a week for very long stretches. In addition to deciding when to work, and for how long, you also need to think about when and where to work. If you are a lark, you will work better early in the day; if you are an owl, you will be at your best later on. Whatever time you work, you need somewhere quiet so that you can concentrate, and with space for books and other resources you need. If the words 'quiet oasis' and 'your house' are totally incompatible at any time of the day or night then check out the opening hours of your local and college library so that you have an escape route if you need it. If you are trying to combine studying with parental responsibilities it is sensible to factor-in your children's commitments – and work around their bedtimes too! Store up favours, too, from friends and parents/grandparents that you can call in if you get desperate for extra time when an assignment deadline is looming.

- **Schedule your commitments** Keep a diary or (even better) a wall chart and write down every appointment you make or task you are given. It is useful to use a colour code to differentiate between personal and work or course commitments. You may also want to enter assignment review dates with your tutor in one colour and final deadline dates in another. Keep your diary or chart up-to-date by adding any new dates promptly every time you receive another task or assignment or whenever you make any other arrangements. Keep checking ahead so that you always have prior warning when important dates are looming. This stops you from planning a heavy social week when you will be at your busiest at work or college and from arranging a dental appointment on the morning when you and your team are scheduled to give an important presentation!

- **Prioritise your work** This means doing the most important and urgent task first, rather than the one you like the most! Normally, this will be the task or assignment with the nearest deadline. There are two exceptions. Sometimes you may need to send off for information and allow time for it to arrive. It is therefore sensible to do this first so that you are not held up later. The second exception is when you have to take account of other people's schedules – because you are working in a team or are arranging to interview someone, for example. In this case you will have to arrange your schedule around their needs, not just your own.

- **Set sensible timescales** Trying to do work at the last minute or in a rush is never satisfactory, so it is always wise to allocate more time than you think you will need, never less. Remember, too, to include all the stages of a complex task or assignment, such as researching the information, deciding what to use, creating a first draft, checking it and making improvements and printing it out. If you are planning to do any of your work in a central facility always allow extra time and try to start work early. If you arrive at the last minute you may find every computer and printer is fully utilised until closing time.

- **Learn self-discipline!** This means not putting things off (procrastinating!) because you don't know where to start or don't feel in the mood. Unless you are ill, you have to find some way of persuading yourself to work. One way is to bribe yourself. Make a start and promise yourself that if you work productively for 30 minutes then you deserve a small reward. After 30 minutes you may have become more engrossed and want to keep going a little longer. Otherwise at least you have made a start, so it's easier to come back and do more later. It doesn't matter whether you have research to do, an assignment to write up, a coaching session to plan, or lines to learn, you need to be self-disciplined.

- **Take regular breaks and keep your life in balance** Don't go to the opposite extreme and work for hours on end. Take regular breaks to give yourself a rest and a change of activity. You need to recharge your batteries! Similarly, don't cancel every social arrangement so that you can work 24/7. Whilst this may be occasionally necessary if you have several deadlines looming simultaneously, it should only be a last resort. If you find yourself doing this regularly then go back to the beginning of this section and see where your time–management planning is going wrong.

PLUSPOINTS

+ Being in control of your time enables you to balance your commitments according to their importance and allows you to not let anyone down – including yourself.

+ Controlling time involves knowing how you spend (and waste!) your time now, planning when best to do work, scheduling your commitments and setting sensible timescales for work to be done.

+ Knowing how to prioritise means that you will schedule work effectively, according to its urgency and importance, but this also requires self-discipline. You have to follow the schedule you have set for yourself!

+ Managing time and focusing on the task at hand means you will do better work and be less stressed, because you are not having to react to problems or crises. You can also find the time to include regular breaks and leisure activities in your schedule.

ACTION POINTS

✓ Find out how many assignments you can expect to receive this term and when you can expect to receive these. Enter this information into your student diary or onto a planner you can refer to regularly.

✓ Update your diary and/or planner with other commitments that you have this term – both work/college-related and social. Identify any potential clashes and decide the best action to take to solve the problem.

✓ Identify your own best time and place to work quietly and effectively.

✓ Displacement activities are things we do to put off starting a job we don't want to do – such as sending texts, watching TV, checking emails etc. Identify yours so that you know when you're doing them!

STEP FOUR

UTILISE ALL YOUR RESOURCES

Your resources are all the things that can help you to achieve your qualification. They can therefore be as wide-ranging as your favourite website and your **study buddy** (see below) who collects handouts for you if you miss a class.

Your college will provide the essential resources for your course, such as a library with a wide range of books and electronic reference sources, learning resource centre(s), the computer network and Internet access. Other basic resources you will be expected to provide yourself, such as file folders and paper. The policy on textbooks varies from one college to another, but today, on most courses, students are expected to buy their own. If you look after yours carefully, then you have the option to sell it on to someone else afterwards and recoup some of your money. If you scribble all over it, leave it on the floor and then tread on it, turn back pages and rapidly turn it into a dog-eared, misshapen version of its former self then you miss out on this opportunity.

Unfortunately, students often squander other opportunities to utilise resources in the best way – usually because they don't think about them very much, if at all. To help, below is a list of the resources you should consider important – with a few tips on how to get the best out of them.

- **Course information** This includes your course specification, this Study Guide and all the other information relating to your BTEC National which you can find on the Edexcel website. Add to this all the information given to you at college relating to your course, including term dates, assignment dates and, of course, your timetable. This should not be 'dead' information that you glance at once and then discard or ignore. Rather, it is important reference material that you need to store somewhere obvious, so that you can look at it whenever you have a query or need to clarify something quickly.

- **Course materials** In this group is your textbook (if there is one), the handouts you are given as well as print-outs and notes you make yourself. File handouts the moment you are given them and put them into an A4 folder bought for the purpose. You will need one for each unit you study. Some students prefer lever-arch files but these are more bulky, so more difficult to carry around all day. Unless you have a locker at college it can be easier to keep a lever-arch file at home for permanent storage of past handouts and notes for a unit, and carry an A4 folder with you which contains current topic information. Filing handouts and print-outs promptly means they don't get lost. They are also less likely to get crumpled, torn or tatty, becoming virtually unreadable. Unless you have a private and extensive source of income then this is even more important if you have to pay for every print-out you take in your college resource centre. If you are following a course such as Art and Design, then there will be all your art materials and the pieces you produce. You must look after these with great care.

- **Other stationery items** Having your own pens, pencils, notepad, punch, stapler and sets of dividers is essential. Nothing irritates tutors more than watching one punch circulate around a group – except, perhaps, the student who trudges into class with nothing to write on or with. Your dividers should be clearly labelled to help you store and find notes, print-outs and handouts fast. Similarly, your notes should be clearly headed and dated. If you are writing-up notes from your own research then you will have to include your source. Researching information is explained in Step 6 – Sharpen your skills.

- **Equipment and facilities** These include your college library and resource centres, the college computer network and other college equipment you can use, such as laptop computers, photocopiers and presentation equipment. Much of this may be freely available; others – such as using the photocopier in the college library or the printers in a resource centre – may cost you money. Many useful resources will be electronic, such as DVDs or electronic journals and databases. At home you may have your own computer with Internet access to count as a resource. Finally, include any specialist equipment and facilities available for your particular course that you use at college or have at home.

Utilise all your resources

All centralised college resources and facilities are invaluable if you know how to use them – but can be baffling when you don't. Your induction should have included how to use the library, resource centre(s) and computer network. You should also have been informed of the policy on using IT equipment, which determines what you can and can't do when you are using college computers. If, by any chance, you missed this then go and check it out for yourself. Library and resource-centre staff will be only too pleased to give you helpful advice – especially if you pick a quiet time to call in. You can also find out about the allowable ways to transfer data between your college computer and your home computer if your options are limited because of IT security.

Having a study buddy is a good idea

- **People** You are surrounded by people who are valuable resources: your tutor(s), specialist staff at college, your employer and work colleagues, your relatives and any friends who have particular skills or who work in the same area you are studying. Other members of your class are also useful resources – although they may not always seem like it! Use them, for example, to discuss topics out of class time. A good debate between a group of students can often raise and clarify issues that there may not be time to discuss fully in class. Having a study buddy is another good idea – you get/make notes for them when they are away and vice versa. That way you don't miss anything.

  If you want information or help from someone, especially anyone outside your immediate circle, then remember to get the basics right! Approach them courteously, do your homework first so that you are well-prepared and remember that you are asking for assistance – not trying to get them to do the work for you! If someone has agreed to allow you to interview them as part of your research for an assignment or project then good preparations will be vital, as you will see in Step 6 – Sharpen your Skills (see page 22).

  One word of warning: be wary about using information from friends or relatives who have done a similar or earlier course. First, the slant of the material they were given may be different. It may also be out-of-date. And *never* copy anyone else's written assignments. This is **plagiarism** – a deadly sin in the educational world. You can read more about this in Step 5 – Understand your assessment (see page 16).

- **You!** You have the ability to be your own best resource or your own worst enemy! The difference depends upon your work skills, your personal skills and your attitude to your course and other people. You have already seen how to use time wisely. Throughout this guide you will find out how to sharpen and improve other work and personal skills and how to get the most out of your course – but it is up to you to read it and apply your new-found knowledge! This is why attributes like a positive attitude, an enquiring mind and the ability to focus on what is important all have a major impact on your final result.

15

PLUSPOINTS

+ Resources help you to achieve your qualification. You will squander these unwittingly if you don't know what they are or how to use them properly.

+ Course information needs to be stored safely for future reference: course materials need to be filed promptly and accurately so that you can find them quickly.

+ You need your own set of key stationery items; you also need to know how to use any central facilities or resources such as the library, learning resource centres and your computer network.

+ People are often a key resource – school or college staff, work colleagues, members of your class, people who are experts in their field.

+ You can be your own best resource! Develop the skills you need to be able to work quickly and accurately and to get the most out of other people who can help you.

ACTION POINTS

✓ Under the same headings as in this section, list all the resources you need for your course and tick-off those you currently have. Then decide how and when you can obtain anything vital that you lack.

✓ Check that you know how to access and use all the shared resources to which you have access at school or college.

✓ Pair-up with someone on your course as a study buddy – and don't let them down!

✓ Test your own storage systems. How fast can you find notes or print-outs you made yesterday/last week/last month – and what condition are they in?

✓ Find out the IT policy at your school or college and make sure you abide by it.

16

STEP FIVE

UNDERSTAND YOUR ASSESSMENT

The key to doing really, really well on any BTEC National course is to understand exactly what you are expected to do in your assignments – and then to do it! It really is as simple as that. So why is it that some people go wrong?

Obviously, you may worry that an assignment may be so difficult that it is beyond you. Actually, this is highly unlikely to happen because all your assignments are based on topics you will have already covered thoroughly in class. Therefore, if you have attended regularly – and have clarified any queries or worries you have, either in class or during your tutorials, this shouldn't happen. If you have had an unavoidably lengthy absence then you may need to review your progress with your tutor and decide how best to cope with the situation. Otherwise, you should note that the main problems with assignments are usually due to far more mundane pitfalls – such as:

✗ not reading the instructions or the assignment brief properly

✗ not understanding what you are supposed to do

✗ only doing part of the task or answering part of a question

✗ skimping the preparation, the research or the whole thing

✗ not communicating your ideas clearly

✗ guessing answers rather than researching properly

✗ padding-out answers with irrelevant information

✗ leaving the work until the last minute and then doing it in a rush

✗ ignoring advice and feedback your tutor has given you.

You can avoid all of these traps by following the guidelines below so that you know exactly what you are doing, prepare well and produce your best work.

The assignment 'brief'

The word 'brief' is just another way of saying 'instructions'. Often, though, a 'brief' (despite its name!) may be rather lengthy. The brief sets the context for the work, defines what evidence you will need to produce and matches the grading criteria to the tasks. It will also give you a schedule for completing the tasks. For example, a brief may include details of a case study you have to read; research you have to carry out or a task you have to do, as well as questions you have to answer. Or it may give you details about a project or group presentation you have to prepare. The type of assignments you receive will depend partly upon the vocational area you are studying, but you can expect some to be in the form of written assignments. Others are likely to be more practical or project-based, especially if you are doing a very practical subject such as Art and Design, Performing Arts or Sport. You may also be assessed in the workplace. For example, this is a course requirement if you are studying Children's Care, Learning and Development.

The assignment brief may also include the **learning outcomes** to which it relates. These tell you the purpose of the assessment and the knowledge you need to demonstrate to obtain a required grade. If your brief doesn't list the learning outcomes, then you should check this information against the unit specification to see the exact knowledge you need to demonstrate.

The grade(s) you can obtain will also be stated on the assignment brief. Sometimes an assignment will focus on just one grade. Others may give you the opportunity to develop or extend your work to progress to a higher grade. This is often dependent upon submitting acceptable work at the previous grade first. You will see examples of this in the Assessed Assignment section of this Study Guide on page 114.

The brief will also tell you if you have to do part of the work as a member of a group. In this case, you must identify your own contribution. You may also be expected to take part in a **peer review**, where you all give feedback on the contribution of one another. Remember that you should do this as objectively and professionally as possible – not just praise everyone madly in the hope that they will do the same for you! In any assignment where there is a group contribution, there is virtually always an individual component, so that your individual grade can be assessed accurately.

Finally, your assignment brief should state the final deadline for handing in the work as well as any interim review dates when you can discuss your progress and ideas with your tutor. These are very important dates indeed and should be entered immediately into your diary or planner. You should schedule your work around these dates so that you have made a start by

17

the first date. This will then enable you to note any queries or significant issues you want to discuss. Otherwise you will waste a valuable opportunity to obtain useful feedback on your progress. Remember, too, to take a notebook to any review meetings so that you can write down the guidance you are given.

Your school or college rules and regulations

Your school or college will have a number of policies and guidelines about assignments and assessment. These will deal with issues such as:

- The procedure you must follow if you have a serious personal problem so cannot meet the deadline date and need an extension.

- Any penalties for missing a deadline date without any good reason.

- The penalties for copying someone else's work (**plagiarism**). These will be severe so make sure that you never share your work (including your CDs) with anyone else and don't ask to borrow theirs.

- The procedure to follow if you are unhappy with the final grade you receive.

Even though it is unlikely that you will ever need to use any of these policies, it is sensible to know they exist, and what they say, just as a safeguard.

Understanding the question or task

There are two aspects to a question or task that need attention. The first are the *command words*, which are explained below. The second are the *presentation instructions*, so that if you are asked to produce a table or graph or report then you do exactly that – and don't write a list or an essay instead!

Command words are used to specify how a question must be answered, eg 'explain', 'describe', 'analyse', 'evaluate'. These words relate to the type of answer required. So whereas you may be asked to 'describe' something at Pass level, you will need to do more (such as 'analyse' or 'evaluate') to achieve Merit or Distinction.

Many students fail to get a higher grade because they do not realise the difference between these words. They simply don't know *how* to analyse or evaluate, so give an explanation instead. Just adding to a list or giving a few more details will never give you a higher grade – instead, you need to change your whole approach to the answer.

The **grading grid** for each unit of your course gives you the command words, so that you can find out exactly what you have to do in each unit, to obtain a Pass, Merit and Distinction. The following charts show you what is usually required when you see a particular command word. You can use this, and the assessed assignments on pages 114–150, to see the difference between the types of answers required for each grade. (The assignments your Centre gives you will be specially written to ensure you have the opportunity to achieve all the possible grades.) Remember, though, that these are just examples to guide you. The exact response will often depend upon the way a question is worded, so if you have any doubts at all check with your tutor before you start work.

There are two other important points to note:

- Sometimes the same command word may be repeated for different grades – such as 'create' or 'explain'. In this case the *complexity* or *range* of the task itself increases at the higher grades – as you will see if you read the grading grid for the unit.

- Command words can also vary depending upon your vocational area. If you are studying Performing Arts or Art and Design you will probably find several command words that an Engineer or IT Practitioner would not – and vice versa!

To obtain a Pass grade

To achieve this grade you must usually demonstrate that you understand the important facts relating to a topic and can state these clearly and concisely.

Command word	What this means
Create (or produce)	Make, invent or construct an item.
Describe	Give a clear, straightforward description that includes all the main points and links these together logically.
Define	Clearly explain what a particular term means and give an example, if appropriate, to show what you mean.
Explain. . .how/why	Set out in detail the meaning of something, with reasons. It is often helpful to give an example of what you mean. Start with the topic, then give the 'how' or 'why'.
Identify	Distinguish and state the main features or basic facts relating to a topic.
Interpret	Define or explain the meaning of something.
Illustrate	Give examples to show what you mean.
List	Provide the information required in a list rather than in continuous writing.
Outline	Write a clear description that includes all the main points, but avoid going into too much detail.
Plan (or devise)	Work out and explain how you would carry out a task or activity.
Select (and present) information	Identify relevant information to support the argument you are making and communicate this in an appropriate way.
State	Write a clear and full account.
Undertake	Carry out a specific activity.
Examples: **Identify** the main features on a digital camera. **Describe** your usual lifestyle. **Outline** the steps to take to carry out research for an assignment.	

19

To obtain a Merit grade

To obtain this grade you must prove that you can apply your knowledge in a specific way.

Command word	What this means
Analyse	Identify separate factors, say how they are related and how each one relates to the topic.
Classify	Sort your information into appropriate categories before presenting or explaining it.
Compare and contrast	Identify the main factors that apply in two or more situations and explain the similarities and differences or advantages and disadvantages.
Demonstrate	Provide several relevant examples or appropriate evidence which support the arguments you are making. In some vocational areas this may also mean giving a practical performance.
Discuss	Provide a thoughtful and logical argument to support the case you are making.
Explain (in detail)	Provide details and give reasons and/or evidence to clearly support the argument you are making.
Implement	Put into practice or operation. You may also have to interpret or justify the effect or result.
Interpret	Understand and explain an effect or result.
Justify	Give appropriate reasons to support your opinion or views and show how you arrived at these conclusions.
Relate/report	Give a full account of, with reasons.
Research	Carry out a full investigation.
Specify	Provide full details and descriptions of selected items or activities.

Examples:

Compare and contrast the performance of two different digital cameras.
Justify your usual lifestyle.
Explain [in detail] the steps to take to research an assignment.

To obtain a Distinction grade

To obtain this grade you must prove that you can make a reasoned judgement based on appropriate evidence.

Command word	What this means
Analyse	Identify the key factors, show how they are linked and explain the importance and relevance of each.
Assess	Give careful consideration to all the factors or events that apply and identify which are the most important and relevant, with reasons for your views.
Comprehensively explain	Give a very detailed explanation that covers all the relevant points and give reasons for your views or actions.
Comment critically	Give your view after you have considered all the evidence, particularly the importance of both the relevant positive and negative aspects.
Evaluate	Review the information and then bring it together to form a conclusion. Give evidence to support each of your views or statements.
Evaluate critically	Review the information to decide the degree to which something is true, important or valuable. Then assess possible alternatives taking into account their strengths and weaknesses if they were applied instead. Then give a precise and detailed account to explain your opinion.
Summarise	Identify and review the main, relevant factors and/or arguments so that these are explained in a clear and concise manner.

Examples:

Assess ten features commonly found on a digital camera.

Evaluate critically your usual lifestyle.

Analyse your own ability to carry out effective research for an assignment.

Responding positively

This is often the most important attribute of all! If you believe that assignments give you the opportunity to demonstrate what you know and how you can apply it *and* positively respond to the challenge by being determined to give it your best shot, then you will do far better than someone who is defeated before they start.

It obviously helps, too, if you are well organised and have confidence in your own abilities – which is what the next section is all about!

PLUSPOINTS

+ Many mistakes in assignments are through errors that can easily be avoided, such as not reading the instructions properly or doing only part of the task that was set!

+ Always read the assignment brief very carefully indeed. Check that you understand exactly what you have to do and the learning outcomes you must demonstrate.

+ Make a note of the deadline for an assignment and any interim review dates on your planner. Schedule work around these dates so that you can make the most of reviews with your tutor.

+ Make sure you know about school or college policies relating to assessment, such as how to obtain an extension or query a final grade.

+ For every assignment, make sure you understand the command words, which tell you how to answer the question, and the presentation instructions, which say what you must produce.

+ Command words are shown in the grading grid for each unit of your qualification. Expect command words and/or the complexity of a task to be different at higher grades, because you have to demonstrate higher-level skills.

ACTION POINTS

✓ Discuss with your tutor the format (style) of assignments you are likely to receive on your course, eg assignments, projects, or practical work where you are observed.

✓ Check the format of the assignments in the Assessed Assignments section of this book. Look at the type of work students did to gain a Pass and then look at the difference in the Merit answers. Read the tutor's comments carefully and ask your own tutor if there is anything you do not understand.

✓ Check out all the policies and guidelines at your school or college that relate to assessment and make sure you understand them.

✓ Check out the grading grid for the units you are currently studying and identify the command words for each grade. Then check you understand what they mean using the explanations above. If there are any words that are not included, ask your tutor to explain the meanings and what you would be required to do.

STEP SIX

SHARPEN YOUR SKILLS

To do your best in any assignment you need a number of skills. Some of these may be vocationally specific, or professional; skills that you are learning as part of your course, such as acting or dancing if you are taking a Performing Arts course or, perhaps, football if you are following a Sports course. Others, though, are broader skills that will help you to do well in assignments no matter what subjects or topics you are studying – such as communicating clearly and co-operating with others.

Some of these skills you will have already and in some areas you may be extremely proficient. Knowing where your weaknesses lie, though, and doing something about them has many benefits. You will work more quickly, more accurately *and* have increased confidence in your own abilities. As an extra bonus, all these skills also make you more effective at work – so there really is no excuse for not giving yourself a quick skills-check and then remedying any problem areas.

This section contains hints and tips to help you check out and improve each of the following areas:

- Your numeracy skills
- Keyboarding and document preparation
- Your IT skills
- Your written communication skills
- Working with others
- Researching information
- Making a presentation.

Your numeracy skills

Some people have the idea that they can ignore numeracy because this skill isn't relevant to their vocational area – such as Art and Design or Children's Care, Learning and Development. If this is how you think then you are wrong! Numeracy is a life skill that everyone needs, so if you can't carry out basic calculations accurately then you will have problems, often when you least expect them.

Fortunately, there are several things you can do to remedy this situation:

- Practise basic calculations in your head and then check them on a calculator.
- Ask your tutor about any essential calculations which give you difficulties.
- Use your onscreen calculator (or a spreadsheet package) to do calculations for you when you are using your computer.
- Try your hand at Sudoku puzzles – either on paper or by using a software package or online at sites such as www.websudoku.com/.
- Investigate puzzle sites and brain training software, such as http://school.discovery.com/brainboosters/ and Dr Kawashima's Brain Training by Nintendo.
- Check out online sites such as www.bbc.co.uk/skillswise/ and www.bbc.co.uk/schools/ks3bitesize/maths/number/index.shtml to improve your skills.

Numeracy is a life skill

Keyboarding and document preparation

- Think seriously about learning to touch-type to save hours of time! Your school or college may have a workshop you can join or you can learn online such as by downloading a free program at www.sense-lang.org/typing/ or practising on sites such as www.computerlab.kids.new.net/keyboarding.htm.
- Obtain correct examples of document formats you will have to use, such as a report or summary. Your tutor may provide you with these or you can find examples in many communication textbooks.
- Proofread work you produce on a computer *carefully*. Remember that your spell checker will not pick up every mistake you make, such as a mistyped word that makes another word (eg form/from; sheer/shear)

and grammar checkers, too, are not without their problems! This means you still have to read your work through yourself. If possible, let your work go 'cold' before you do this so that you read it afresh and don't make assumptions about what you have written. Then read word-by-word to make sure it still makes sense and there are no silly mistakes, such as missing or duplicated words.

■ Make sure your work looks professional by using an appropriate typeface and font size as well as suitable margins.

■ Print-out your work carefully and store it neatly, so it looks in pristine condition when you hand it in.

Your IT skills

■ Check that you can use the main features of all the software packages that you will need to produce your assignments, such as Word, Excel and PowerPoint.

■ Adopt a good search engine, such as Google, and learn to use it properly. Many have online tutorials such as www.googleguide.com.

■ Develop your IT skills to enable you to enhance your assignments appropriately. For example, this may include learning how to import and export text and artwork from one package to another; taking digital photographs and inserting them into your work and/or creating drawings or diagrams by using appropriate software for your course.

Your written communication skills

A poor vocabulary will reduce your ability to explain yourself clearly; work peppered with spelling or punctuation errors looks unprofessional.

■ Read more. This introduces you to new words and familiarises you over and over again with the correct way to spell words.

■ Look up words you don't understand in a dictionary and then try to use them yourself in conversation.

■ Use the Thesaurus in Word to find alternatives to words you find yourself regularly repeating, to add variety to your work.

■ *Never* use words you don't understand in the hope that they sound impressive!

■ Do crosswords to improve your word power and spelling.

■ Resolve to master punctuation – especially apostrophes – either by using an online programme or working your way through the relevant section of a communication textbook that you like.

■ Check out online sites such as www.bbc.co.uk/skillswise/ and www.bbc. co.uk/schools/gcsebitesize/english/ as well as puzzle sites with communication questions such as http://school.discovery.com/brainboosters/.

Working with others

In your private life you can choose who you want to be with and how you respond to them. At work you cannot do that – you are paid to be professional and this means working alongside a wide variety of people, some of whom you may like and some of whom you may not!

The same applies at school or college. By the time you have reached BTEC National level you will be expected to have outgrown wanting to work with your best friends on every project! You may not be very keen on everyone who is in the same team as you, but – at the very least – you can be pleasant, co-operative and helpful. In a large group this isn't normally too difficult. You may find it much harder if you have to partner someone who has very different ideas and ways of working to you.

In this case it may help if you:

- Realise that everyone is different and that your ways of working may not always be the best!

- Are prepared to listen and contribute to a discussion (positively) in equal amounts. Make sure, too, that you encourage the quiet members of the group to speak up by asking them what their views are. The ability to draw other people into the discussion is an important and valuable skill to learn.

- Write down what you have said you will do, so that you don't forget anything.

- Are prepared to do your fair share of the work.

- Discuss options and alternatives with people – don't give them orders or meekly accept instructions and then resent it afterwards.

- Don't expect other people to do what you wouldn't be prepared to do.

- Are sensitive to other people's feelings and remember that they may have personal problems or issues that affect their behaviour.

- *Always* keep your promises and never let anyone down when they are depending upon you.

- Don't flounce around or lose your temper if things get tough. Instead, take a break while you cool down. Then sit down and discuss the issues that are annoying you.

- Help other people to reach a compromise when necessary, by acting as peacemaker.

Researching information

Poor researchers either cannot find what they want or find too much – and then 'drown' in a pile of papers. If you find yourself drifting aimlessly around a library when you want information or printing-out dozens of pages for no apparent purpose, then this section is for you!

- Always check *exactly* what it is you need to find and how much detail is needed. Write down a few key words to keep yourself focused.

- Discipline yourself to ignore anything that is irrelevant – from books with interesting titles to websites which sound tempting but have little to do with your topic or key words.

- Remember that you could theoretically research information forever! So at some time you have to call a halt. Learning when to do this is another skill, but you can learn this by writing out a schedule which clearly states when you have to stop looking, and start sorting out your information and writing about it!

- In a library, check you know how the books are stored and what other types of media are available. If you can't find what you are looking for then ask the librarian for help. Checking the index in a book is the quickest way to find out whether it contains information related to your key words. Put it back if it doesn't or if you can't understand it. If you find three or four books and/or journals that contain what you need then that is usually enough.

- Online, use a good search engine and use the summary of the search results to check out the best sites. Force yourself to check-out sites beyond page one of the search results! When you enter a site, investigate it carefully – use the site map if necessary. It isn't always easy to find exactly what you want. Bookmark sites you find helpful and will want to use again and only take print-outs when the information is closely related to your key words.

- Talk to people who can help you (see also Step 4 – Utilise all your resources) and prepare in advance by thinking about the best questions to ask. Always explain why you want the information and don't expect anyone to tell you anything that is confidential or sensitive – such as personal information or financial details. Always write clear notes so that you remember what you have been told, by whom and when. If you are wise you will also note down their contact details so that you can contact them again if you think of anything later. If you remember to be courteous and thank them for their help, this shouldn't be a problem.

- Store all your precious information carefully and neatly in a labelled folder so that you can find it easily. Then, when you are ready to start work, reread it and extract that which is most closely related to your key words and the task you are doing.

- Make sure you state the source of all the information you quote by including the name of the author or the web address, either in the text or as part of a bibliography at the end. Your school or college will have a help sheet which will tell you exactly how to do this.

Making a presentation

This involves several skills – which is why it is such a popular way of finding out what students can do! It will test your ability to work in a team, speak in public and use IT (normally PowerPoint) – as well as your nerves. It is therefore excellent practice for many of the tasks you will have to do when you are at work – from attending an interview to talking to an important client.

You will be less nervous if you have prepared well and have rehearsed your role beforehand. You will produce a better, more professional presentation if you take note of the following points.

- If you are working as a team, work out everyone's strengths and weaknesses and divide up the work (fairly) taking these into account. Work out, too, how long each person should speak and who would be the best as the 'leader' who introduces each person and then summarises everything at the end.

PLUSPOINTS

+ Poor numeracy skills can let you down in your assignments and at work. Work at improving these if you regularly struggle with even simple calculations.

+ Good keyboarding, document production and IT skills can save you hours of time and mean that your work is of a far more professional standard. Improve any of these areas which are letting you down.

+ Your written communication skills will be tested in many assignments. Work at improving areas of weakness, such as spelling, punctuation or vocabulary.

+ You will be expected to work co-operatively with other people, both at work and during many assignments. Be sensitive to other people's feelings, not just your own, and always be prepared to do your fair share of the work and help other people when you can.

+ To research effectively you need to know exactly what you are trying to find and where to look. This means understanding how reference media is stored in your library as well as how to search online. Good organisation skills also help so that you store important information carefully and can find it later. And never forget to include your sources in a bibliography.

+ Making a presentation requires several skills and may be nerve-racking at first. You will reduce your problems if you prepare well, are not too ambitious and have several run-throughs beforehand. Remember to speak clearly and a little more slowly than normal and smile from time to time!

ACTION POINTS

✓ Test both your numeracy and literacy skills at http://www.move-on.org.uk/testyourskills.asp# to check your current level. You don't need to register on the site if you click to do the 'mini-test' instead. If either need improvement, get help at http://www.bbc.co.uk/keyskills/it/1.shtml.

✓ Do the following two tasks with a partner to jerk your brain into action!

- Each write down 36 simple calculations in a list, eg 8 x 6, 19 – 8, 14 + 6. Then exchange lists. See who can answer the most correctly in the shortest time.

- Each write down 30 short random words (no more than 8 letters), eg cave, table, happily. Exchange lists. You each have three minutes to try to remember as many words as possible. Then hand back the list and write down all those you can recall. See who can remember the most.

✓ Assess your own keyboarding, proof-reading, document production, written communication and IT skills. Then find out if your tutors agree with you!

✓ List ten traits in other people that drive you mad. Then, for each one, suggest what you could do to cope with the problem (or solve it) rather than make a fuss. Compare your ideas with other members of your group.

✓ Take a note of all feedback you receive from your tutors, especially in relation to working with other people, researching and giving presentations. In each case focus on their suggestions and ideas so that you continually improve your skills throughout the course.

■ Don't be over-ambitious. Take account of your time-scale, resources and the skills of the team. Remember that a simple, clear presentation is often more professional than an over-elaborate or complicated one where half the visual aids don't work properly!

■ If you are using PowerPoint try to avoid preparing every slide with bullet points! For variety, include some artwork and vary the designs. Remember that you should *never* just read your slides to the audience! Instead, prepare notes that you can print-out that will enable you to enhance and extend what the audience is reading.

- Your preparations should also include checking the venue and time; deciding what to wear and getting it ready; preparing, checking and printing any handouts; deciding what questions might be asked and how to answer these.

- Have several run-throughs beforehand and check your timings. Check, too, that you can be heard clearly. This means lifting up your head and 'speaking' to the back of the room a little more slowly and loudly than you normally do.

- On the day, arrive in plenty of time so that you aren't rushed or stressed. Remember that taking deep breaths helps to calm your nerves.

- Start by introducing yourself clearly and smile at the audience. If it helps, find a friendly face and pretend you are just talking to that person.

- Answer any questions honestly and don't exaggerate, guess or waffle. If you don't know the answer then say so!

- If you are giving the presentation in a team, help out someone else who is struggling with a question if you know the answer.

- Don't get annoyed or upset if you get any negative feedback afterwards. Instead, take note so that you can concentrate on improving your own performance next time. And don't focus on one or two criticisms and ignore all the praise you received! Building on the good and minimising the bad is how everyone improves in life!

STEP SEVEN

MAXIMISE YOUR OPPORTUNITIES AND MANAGE YOUR PROBLEMS

Like most things in life, you may have a few ups-and-downs on your course – particularly if you are studying over quite a long time, such as one or two years. Sometimes everything will be marvellous – you are enjoying all the units, you are up-to-date with your work, you are finding the subjects interesting and having no problems with any of your research tasks. At other times you may struggle a little more. You may find one or two topics rather tedious, or there may be distractions or worries in your personal life that you have to cope with. You may struggle to concentrate on the work and do your best.

Rather than just suffering in silence or gritting your teeth if things go a bit awry it is sensible if you have an action plan to help you cope. Equally, rather than just accepting good opportunities for additional experiences or learning, it is also wise to plan how to make the best of these. This section will show you how to do this.

Making the most of your opportunities

The following are examples of opportunities to find out more about information relevant to your course or to try putting some of your skills into practice.

- **External visits** You may go out of college on visits to different places or organisations. These are not days off – there is a reason for making each trip. Prepare in advance by reading around relevant topics and make notes of useful information whilst you are there. Then write (or type) it up neatly as soon as you can and file it where you can find it again!

- **Visiting speakers** Again, people are asked to talk to your group for a purpose. You are likely to be asked to contribute towards questions that may be asked – which may be submitted in advance so that the speaker is clear on the topics you are studying. Think carefully about information that you would find helpful so that you can ask one or two relevant and useful questions. Take notes whilst the speaker is addressing your group, unless someone is recording the session. Be prepared to thank the speaker on behalf of your group if you are asked to do so.

- **Professional contacts** These will be the people you meet on work experience doing the real job that one day you hope to do. Make the most of meeting these people to find out about the vocational area of your choice.

- **Work experience** If you need to undertake practical work for any particular units of your BTEC National qualification, and if you are studying full-time, then your tutor will organise a work-experience placement for you and talk to you about the evidence you need to obtain. You may also be issued with a special log book or diary in which to record your experiences. Before you start your placement, check that you are clear about all the details, such as the time you will start and leave, the name of your supervisor, what you should wear and what you should do if you are ill during the placement and cannot attend. Read and reread the units to which your evidence will apply and make sure you understand the grading criteria and what you need to obtain. Then make a note of appropriate headings to record your information. Try to make time to write-up your notes, log book and/or diary every night, whilst your experiences are fresh in your mind.

- **In your own workplace** You may be studying your BTEC National qualification on a part-time basis and also have a full-time job in the same vocational area. Or you may be studying full-time and have a part-time job just to earn some money. In either case you should be alert to opportunities to find out more about topics that relate to your workplace, no matter how generally. For example, many BTEC courses include topics such as health and safety, teamwork, dealing with customers, IT security and communications – to name but a few. All these are topics that your employer will have had to address and finding out more about these will broaden your knowledge and help to give more depth to your assignment responses.

- **Television programmes, newspapers, Podcasts and other information sources** No matter what vocational area you are studying, the media are likely to be an invaluable source of information. You should be alert to any news bulletins that relate to your studies as well as relevant information in more topical television programmes. For example, if you are studying Art and Design then you should make a particular effort to watch the *Culture Show* as well as programmes on artists, exhibitions or other topics of interest. Business students should find inspiration by watching *Dragons Den*, *The Apprentice* and *The Money Programme* and Travel and Tourism students should watch holiday, travel and adventure programmes. If you are studying Media, Music and Performing Arts then you are spoiled for choice! Whatever your vocational choice, there will be television and radio programmes of special interest to you.

Remember that you can record television programmes to watch later if you prefer, and check out newspaper headlines online and from sites such as BBC news. The same applies to Podcasts. Of course, to know which information is relevant means that you must be familiar with the content of all the units you are studying, so it is useful to know what topics you will be learning about in the months to come, as well as the ones you are covering now. That way you can recognise useful opportunities when they arise.

The media are invaluable sources of information

Minimising problems

If you are fortunate, any problems you experience on your course will only be minor ones. For example, you may struggle to keep yourself motivated every single day and there may be times that you are having difficulty with a topic. Or you may be struggling to work with someone else in your team or to understand a particular tutor.

During induction you should have been told which tutor to talk to in this situation, and who to see if that person is absent, or if you would prefer to see someone else. If you are having difficulties which are distracting you and affecting your work then it is sensible to ask to see your tutor promptly so that you can talk in confidence, rather than just trusting to luck that everything will go right again. It is a rare student who is madly enthusiastic about every part of a course and all the other people on the course, so your tutor won't be surprised and will be able to give you useful guidance to help you stay on track.

If you are very unlucky, you may have a more serious personal problem to deal with. In this case it is important that you know the main sources of help in your school or college and how to access these.

- **Professional counselling** There may be a professional counselling service if you have a concern that you don't want to discuss with any teaching staff. If you book an appointment to see a counsellor then you can be certain that nothing you say will ever be mentioned to another member of staff without your permission.

- **Student complaints procedures** If you have a serious complaint to make then the first step is to talk to a tutor, but you should be aware of the formal student complaints procedures that exist if you cannot resolve the problem informally. Note that these are only used for serious issues, not for minor difficulties.

- **Student appeals procedures** If you cannot agree with a tutor about a final grade for an assignment then you need to check the grading criteria and ask the tutor to explain how the grade was awarded. If you are still unhappy then you should see your personal tutor. If you still disagree then you have the right to make a formal appeal.

- **Student disciplinary procedures** These exist so that all students who flout the rules in a school or college will be dealt with in the same way. Obviously, it is wise to avoid getting into trouble at any time, but if you find yourself on the wrong side of the regulations then you should read the procedures carefully to see what could happen. Remember that being honest about what happened and making a swift apology is always the wisest course of action, rather than being devious or trying to blame someone else.

■ **Serious illness** Whether this affects you or a close family member, it could severely affect your attendance. The sooner you discuss the problem with your tutor the better. This is because you will be missing notes and information from the first day you do not attend. Many students under-estimate the ability of their tutors to find inventive solutions in this type of situation – from sending notes by post to updating you electronically if you are well enough to cope with the work.

PLUSPOINTS

+ Some students miss-out on opportunities to learn more about relevant topics. This may be because they haven't read the unit specifications, so don't know what topics they will be learning about in future; haven't prepared in advance or don't take advantage of occasions when they can listen to an expert and perhaps ask questions. Examples of these occasions include external visits, visiting speakers, work experience, being at work and watching television.

+ Many students encounter minor difficulties, especially if their course lasts a year or two. It is important to talk to your tutor, or another appropriate person, promptly if you have a worry that is affecting your work.

+ All schools and colleges have procedures for dealing with important issues and problems such as serious complaints, major illnesses, student appeals and disciplinary matters. It is important to know what these are.

ACTION POINTS

✓ List the type of opportunities available on your course for obtaining more information and talking to experts. Then check with your tutor to make sure you haven't missed out any.

✓ Check out the content of each unit you will be studying so that you know the main topics you have still to study.

✓ Identify the type of information you can find on television, in newspapers and in Podcasts that will be relevant to your studies.

✓ Check-out your school or college documents and procedures to make sure that you know who to talk to in a crisis and who you can see if the first person is absent.

✓ Find out where you can read a copy of the main procedures in your school or college that might affect you if you have a serious problem. Then do so.

AND FINALLY . . .

Don't expect this Introduction to be of much use if you skim through it quickly and then put it to one side. Instead, refer to it whenever you need to remind yourself about something related to your course.

The same applies to the rest of this Student Guide. The Activities in the next section have been written to help you to demonstrate your understanding of many of the key topics contained in the core or specialist units you are studying. Your tutor may tell you to do these at certain times; otherwise there is nothing to stop you working through them yourself!

Similarly, the Assessed Assignments in the final section have been written to show you how your assignments may be worded. You can also see the type of response that will achieve a Pass, Merit and Distinction – as well as the type of response that won't! Read these carefully and if any comment or grade puzzles you, ask your tutor to explain it.

Keep this guide in a safe place so that you can use it whenever you need to refresh your memory. That way, you will get the very best out of your course – and yourself!

GLOSSARY

Note: all words highlighted in bold in the text are defined in the glossary.

Accreditation of Prior Learning (APL)

APL is an assessment process that enables your previous achievements and experiences to count towards your qualification providing your evidence is authentic, current, relevant and sufficient.

Apprenticeships

Schemes that enable you to work and earn money at the same time as you gain further qualifications (an **NVQ** award and a technical certificate) and improve your key skills. Apprentices learn work-based skills relevant to their job role and their chosen industry. You can find out more at www.apprenticeships.org.uk/

Assessment methods

Methods, such as **assignments**, case studies and practical tasks, used to check that your work demonstrates the learning and understanding required for your qualification.

Assessor

The tutor who marks or assesses your work.

Assignment

A complex task or mini-project set to meet specific **grading criteria**.

Awarding body

The organisation which is responsible for devising, assessing and issuing qualifications. The awarding body for all BTEC qualifications is Edexcel.

Core units

On a BTEC National course these are the compulsory or mandatory units that all students must complete to gain the qualification. Some BTEC qualifications have an overarching title, eg Engineering, but within Engineering you can choose different routes. In this case you will study both common core units that are common to all engineering qualifications and **specialist core unit(s)** which are specific to your chosen **pathway**.

Degrees

These are higher education qualifications which are offered by universities and colleges. Foundation degrees take two years to complete; honours degrees may take three years or longer. See also **Higher National Certificates and Diplomas**.

DfES

The Department for Education and Skills: this is the government department responsible for education issues. You can find out more at www.dfes.gov.uk

Distance learning

This enables you to learn and/or study for a qualification without attending an Edexcel centre, although you would normally be supported by a member of staff who works there. You communicate with your tutor and/or the centre that organises the distance learning programme by post, telephone or electronically.

Educational Maintenance Award (EMA)

This is a means-tested award which provides eligible students under 19, who are studying a full-time course at school or college, with a cash sum of money every week. See http://www.dfes.gov.uk/financialhelp/ema/ for up-to-date details.

External verification

Formal checking by a representative of Edexcel of the way a BTEC course is delivered. This includes sampling various assessments to check content and grading.

Final major project

This is a major, individual piece of work that is designed to enable you to demonstrate you have achieved several learning outcomes for a BTEC National qualification in the creative or performing arts. Like all assessments, this is internally assessed.

Forbidden combinations

Qualifications or units that cannot be taken simultaneously because their content is too similar.

GLH

See **Guided Learning Hours** below.

Grade

The rating (Pass, Merit or Distinction) given to the mark you have obtained which identifies the standard you have achieved.

Grade boundaries

The pre-set points at which the total points you have earned for different units converts to the overall grade(s) for your qualification.

Grading criteria

The standard you have to demonstrate to obtain a particular grade in the unit, in other words, what you have to prove you can do.

Grading domains

The main areas of learning which support the **learning outcomes**. On a BTEC National course these are: application of knowledge and understanding; development of practical and technical skills; personal development for occupational roles; application of generic and **key skills**. Generic skills are basic skills needed wherever you work, such as the ability to work co-operatively as a member of a team.

Grading grid

The table in each unit of your BTEC qualification specification that sets out the **grading criteria**.

Guided Learning Hours (GLH)

The approximate time taken to deliver a unit, which includes the time taken for direct teaching, instruction and assessment and for you to carry out directed assignments or directed individual study. It does not include any time you spend on private study or researching an assignment. The GLH determines the size of the unit. At BTEC National level, units are either 30, 60, 90 or 120 guided learning hours. By looking at the number of GLH a unit takes, you can see the size of the unit and how long it is likely to take you to learn and understand the topics it contains.

Higher education (HE)

Post-secondary and post-further education, usually provided by universities and colleges.

Higher level skills

Skills such as evaluating or critically assessing complex information that are more difficult than lower level skills such as writing a description or making out a list. You must be able to demonstrate higher level skills to achieve a Distinction grade.

Higher National Certificates and Diplomas

Higher National Certificates and Diplomas are vocational qualifications offered at colleges around the country. Certificates are part-time and designed to be studied by people who are already in work; students can use their work experiences to build on their learning. Diplomas are full-time courses – although often students will spend a whole year on work experience part way through their Diploma. Higher Nationals are roughly equivalent to half a degree.

Indicative reading

Recommended books and journals whose content is both suitable and relevant for the unit.

Induction

A short programme of events at the start of a course designed to give you essential information and introduce you to your fellow students and tutors so that you can settle down as quickly and easily as possible.

Internal verification

The quality checks carried out by nominated tutor(s) at your school or college to ensure that all assignments are at the right level and cover appropriate learning outcomes. The checks also ensure that all **assessors** are marking work consistently and to the same standard.

Investors in People (IIP)

A national quality standard which sets a level of good practice for the training and development of people. Organisations must demonstrate their commitment to achieve the standard.

Key skills

The transferable, essential skills you need both at work and to run your own life successfully. They are: literacy, numeracy, IT, problem solving, working with others and self-management.

Learning and Skills Council (LSC)

The government body responsible for planning and funding education and training for everyone aged over 16 in England – except university students. You can find out more at www.lsc.gov.uk

Learning outcomes

The knowledge and skills you must demonstrate to show that you have effectively learned a unit.

Learning support

Additional help that is available to all students in a school or college who have learning difficulties or other special needs. These include reasonable adjustments to help to reduce the effect of a disability or difficulty that would place a student at a substantial disadvantage in an assessment situation.

Levels of study

The depth, breadth and complexity of knowledge, understanding and skills required to achieve a qualification determines its level. Level 2 is broadly equivalent to GCSE level (grades A*-C) and level 3 equates to GCE level. As you successfully achieve one level, you can then progress on to the next. BTEC qualifications are offered at Entry level, then levels 1, 2, 3, 4 and 5.

Local Education Authority (LEA)

The local government body responsible for providing education for students of compulsory school age in your area.

Mentor

A more experienced person who will guide and counsel you if you have a problem or difficulty.

Mode of delivery

The way in which a qualification is offered to students, eg part-time, full-time, as a short course or by **distance learning**.

National Occupational Standard (NOS)

These are statements of the skills, knowledge and understanding you need to develop to be competent at a particular job. These are drawn up by the **Sector Skills Councils**.

National Qualification Framework (NQF)

The framework into which all accredited qualifications in the UK are placed. Each is awarded a level based on their difficulty which ensures that all those at the same level are of the same standard. (See also **levels of study.**)

National Vocational Qualification (NVQ)

Qualifications which concentrate upon the practical skills and knowledge required to do a job competently. They are usually assessed in the workplace and range from level 1 (the lowest) to level 5 (the highest).

Nested qualifications

Qualifications which have 'common' units, so that students can easily progress from one to another by adding-on more units, such as the BTEC Award, BTEC Certificate and BTEC Diploma.

Pathway

All BTEC National qualifications are comprised of a small number of core units and a larger number of specialist units. These specialist units are grouped into different combinations to provide alternative pathways to achieving the qualification, linked to different career preferences.

Peer review

An occasion when you give feedback on the performance of other members in your team and they, in turn, comment on your performance.

Plagiarism

The practice of copying someone else's work and passing it off as your own. *This is strictly forbidden on all courses.*

Portfolio

A collection of work compiled by a student, usually as evidence of learning to produce for an **assessor**.

Professional body

An organisation that exists to promote or support a particular profession, such as the Law Society and the Royal Institute of British Architects.

Professional development and training

Activities that you can undertake, relevant to your job, that will increase and/or update your knowledge and skills.

Project

A comprehensive piece of work which normally involves original research and investigation either by an individual or a team. The findings and results may be presented in writing and summarised in a presentation.

Qualifications and Curriculum Authority (QCA)

The public body, sponsored by the **DfES**, responsible for maintaining and developing the national curriculum and associated assessments, tests and examinations. It also accredits and monitors qualifications in colleges and at work. You can find out more at www.qca.gov.uk

Quality assurance

In education, this is the process of continually checking that a course of study is meeting the specific requirements set down by the awarding body.

Sector Skills Councils (SSCs)

The 25 employer-led, independent organisations that are responsible for improving workforce skills in the UK by identifying skill gaps and improving learning in the workplace. Each council covers a different type of industry and develops its **National Occupational Standards**.

Semester

Many universities and colleges divide their academic year into two halves or semesters, one from September to January and one from February to July.

Seminar

A learning event between a group of students and a tutor. This may be student-led, following research into a topic which has been introduced earlier.

Specialist core units

See under **Core units**.

Study buddy

A person in your group or class who takes notes for you and keeps you informed of important developments if you are absent. You do the same in return.

Time-constrained assignment

An assessment you must complete within a fixed time limit.

Tutorial

An individual or small group meeting with your tutor at which you can discuss the work you are currently doing and other more general course issues. At an individual tutorial your progress on the course will be discussed and you can also raise any concerns or personal worries you have.

The University and Colleges Admissions Service (UCAS)

The central organisation which processes all applications for higher education courses. You pronounce this 'You-Cass'.

UCAS points

The number of points allocated by **UCAS** for the qualifications you have obtained. **HE** institutions specify how many points you need to be accepted on the courses they offer. You can find out more at www.ucas.com

Unit abstract

The summary at the start of each BTEC unit that tells you what the unit is about.

Unit content

Details about the topics covered by the unit and the knowledge and skills you need to complete it.

Unit points

The number of points you have gained when you complete a unit. These depend upon the grade you achieve (Pass, Merit or Distinction) and the size of the unit as determined by its **guided learning hours**.

Vocational qualification

A qualification which is designed to develop the specific knowledge and understanding relevant to a chosen area of work.

Work experience

Any time you spend on an employer's premises when you carry out work-based tasks as an employee but also learn about the enterprise and develop your skills and knowledge.

ACTIVITIES

This unit focuses on grading criteria P1, P2, P4, P5; M1, M3; and D2.

Unit overview

Whether you are taking a holiday, a short break, a day trip or a business trip, there will be many different types of organisations contributing to your travel and tourism experience. Knowing the components and how they work together will provide a useful foundation for your studies of the travel and tourism industry.

Learning outcomes

1 Know the components of travel and tourism and how they interrelate

3 Understand how recent developments have shaped the present day travel and tourism industry

4 Understand the trends and factors affecting the development of travel and tourism

Content

1) Know the components of travel and tourism and how they interrelate

Components of travel and tourism: accommodation (serviced, non-serviced); transport provision (road, rail, sea, air); attractions (natural, heritage, purpose-built, events); tour operations (mass market, specialist); travel agents (retail, business, call centre, online); tourism development and promotion, eg tourist boards; trade associations and regulatory bodies, eg Association of Independent Tour Operators; ancillary services, eg insurance

Interrelate: chains of distribution; integration; interdependencies

Types of tourism: domestic; inbound; outbound.

3) Understand how recent developments have shaped the present day travel and tourism industry

Recent developments: from the 1960s to the present day, eg legislation, product development, destination development, technological development, transport development, lifestyle changes

Present day travel and tourism industry: eg products and services, business operations, consumer demand, types of organisations, competition, numbers employed in travel and tourism industry, contribution to countries' gross domestic product (GDP).

4) Understand the trends and factors affecting the development of travel and tourism

Trends: eg increased frequency of holidays, greater flexibility (of booking, of products), more independent travellers, adventure travel, new destinations, growth and expansion of regional airports

Factors: eg natural disasters, health warnings and epidemics, terrorism, environmental issues, cost of travel

Development: eg new products and services, retail and business travel operations, consumer demand, distribution methods.

Grading criteria

P1 describe (giving examples including domestic, inbound and outbound tourism) the components of the travel and tourism industry

You will need to describe all of the components of travel and tourism and show that you understand the nature of inbound, outbound and domestic tourism. To support your description and demonstrate your understanding, you will need to give named examples of each of the components you describe. (You do not need to give an example of inbound, outbound and domestic for each component, but all three must be covered across the components.)

P2 describe the ways that components of travel and tourism interrelate

You will need to provide up-to-date information on how different components interrelate, showing typical chains of distribution and describing the different types of integration and how these are applied in the travel and tourism industry.

For both of these criteria, you need to 'describe' what you find; this is about more than just identifying and listing your findings.

P4 describe four recent developments (from the 1960s onwards) that have shaped the present day travel and tourism industry

You can select at least four developments of your choice as long as they have had, or continue to have, an effect on the industry today. You should be careful not to include specific events such as acts of terrorism or natural disasters as 'developments'.

P5 describe three key trends and three factors that are affecting or are likely to affect the development of travel and tourism

At least three key trends and three factors should be described and they should be key to developments occurring currently in the industry or likely to impact on the industry in the future.

M1 explain how the components of travel and tourism interrelate, giving examples that include domestic, inbound and outbound tourism

This will be a detailed description, showing that you have an in-depth understanding of how and why different components interrelate. Your explanation should be supported by up-to-date examples, including domestic, inbound and outbound tourism. A typical example could be a package holiday organised by an inbound tour operator, with an explanation of how accommodation, transport providers, attractions, tourist boards and trade associations work together.

M3 explain how recent developments have shaped the present day travel and tourism industry and how key trends and factors are likely to shape the industry in the future

You must demonstrate that you are able to link how recent developments have affected the travel and tourism industry. You should also be able to demonstrate consideration of how the trends and factors you have chosen may affect the development of the industry.

D2 recommend and justify how the travel and tourism industry could respond to key trends and factors affecting the future development of travel and tourism

You must offer recommendations as to how the industry could adapt to trends and factors. These must be described in some detail and justified by explaining how they will prepare selected organisations, sectors, or the industry as a whole, to deal with identified trends.

COMPONENTS OF TRAVEL AND TOURISM

ACTIVITY 1

Most of our holiday and leisure experiences are the result of the combined efforts of a variety of organisations. Day trips, short breaks, holidays and business trips are made up of different components of travel and tourism which interrelate to provide us with our final 'product'.

Let's consider that you might be presented with the opportunity to go on a school or college trip to *The Deep* in Hull or *The Eden Project* in Cornwall. On the face of it such trips might seem to be quite straightforward, but if you take a look behind the scenes there are many different components of the travel and tourism industry involved in helping to make your trip a reality.

Firstly consider *The Deep* and *The Eden Project* themselves:

The Deep is billed as 'the world's only submarium' and *The Eden Project* has been likened to 'a green theme park'. Both have become highly successful visitor attractions.

New attractions such as these don't just 'happen'. There will have been many organisations involved in their initial development and then in their subsequent promotion, operation and ongoing development.

In addition, the opening of such high-profile attractions will provide opportunities for other travel and tourism organisations to benefit – for example, creating links with transport and accommodation providers, tour operators, guiding services and travel agents.

Task 1

Divide into two groups; one to carry out research into *The Deep* and the other to carry out research into *The Eden Project*.

Find out what the attractions have to offer the visitor, plus:

- How the attractions were funded; which organisations were (and maybe still are) involved in funding the projects
- Links with national and regional tourist boards

41

- Links with tour operators; find an example of a domestic tour operator that includes the attraction in their advertised programme
- Links with coach operators; find an example of a domestic coach operator offering day trips to the attraction
- Links with rail operators; find an example of a rail operator offering special fares or promotions to include the attraction
- Links with accommodation providers; find examples of accommodation providers using the attraction within their promotional materials.

Task 2

For your attraction, produce a large diagram showing the links with different types of organisations. Present your attraction to the other group.

On your own, compare the links for the two attractions and highlight similarities and differences. Make some brief notes for your file.

You will have found from this activity that attractions such as *The Deep* and *The Eden Project* do not work in isolation. They are reliant on many 'partners' for their ongoing success.

ACTIVITY 2

Inbound, domestic and outbound tour operators provide excellent examples of how different components of travel and tourism interrelate.

A typical chain of distribution looks like this:

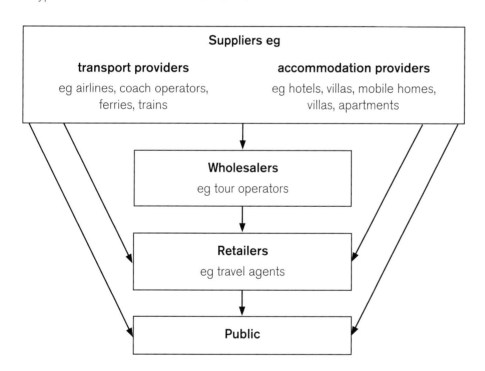

In this chain of distribution, suppliers such as airlines and hotels have choices. They can sell their products direct to the public – for example, via the Internet – or they may use the services of a retailer, like a travel agent. Alternatively, they can make a contract with a tour operator who will act as a wholesaler and put two (or more) components together into a 'package' and sell them at an inclusive price either via a travel agent or direct to the public.

Some travel and tourism organisations are 'vertically integrated', meaning that they own companies at different levels in the chain of distribution – for example, a tour operator that is part of an organisation that also owns an airline and/or a retail travel agency.

Some travel and tourism organisations are horizontally integrated, meaning that they own different companies at the same level in the chain of distribution – for example, an organisation that owns a number of different tour operators.

Some travel and tourism organisations are both vertically and horizontally integrated.

Task 1

Make up your own definitions of the terms 'vertical' and 'horizontal' integration.

Carry out some research into a vertically and horizontally integrated company like Thomas Cook or TUI. Complete a chain of distribution for your chosen company.

As a group, discuss the benefits for a company to be vertically and/or horizontally integrated and how vertical and/or horizontal integration might affect the way that different organisations work together in the travel and tourism industry.

Task 2

Have you ever been on a package holiday?

According to the *Package Travel, Package Holidays and Package Tours Regulations 1992*, a package is defined as:

> ... a pre-arranged holiday combination sold or offered for sale at an inclusive price, covering a period of more than 24 hours and including at least two of the following:
> - transport
> - accommodation
> - other significant tourist services (not ancillary to transport or accommodation).

Tour operators are responsible for putting together most package holidays.

Find out the difference between a domestic, an inbound and an outbound tour operator.

Imagine you have just won £1500 for you and a friend or relative to spend on a package holiday. Have a look through some tour operators' brochures and find the complete package that you would like to take. By 'complete', this means all of your travel, accommodation and 'extras'.

Produce a flowchart to show how the different components of travel and tourism will interrelate, from making your booking and through all the stages of your holiday. As far as you are able, name the different organisations that would be providing you with your selected holiday arrangements.

Compare your flowchart with other members of the class to see if you have missed out any vital components.

Task 3

The travel and tourism industry is dynamic and is constantly changing due to new developments, mergers and acquisitions.

In early 2007 two significant developments in the industry were announced.

Look at these two travel trade headlines, both taken from the *Travel Trade Gazette*, a weekly publication for people working in the travel and tourism industry:

COOKTAIL MIX!

Massive merger of Thomas Cook and MyTravel ….
The merger marks a massive shake up of the UK travel industry, consolidating the big four into three.
The new company, Thomas Cook plc, also replaces Thomson as market leader.

TTG 16 February 2007

AND THEN THERE WERE TWO!

TUI and First Choice merger heralds huge shake up for travel trade.

TTG 23 March 2007

Find out what is meant by the 'big four' as mentioned in the first headline.

Carry out some research to find out more about the stories behind these two headlines.

Discuss what impact these developments might have on other organisations in the travel and tourism industry.

You should try to read *Travel Trade Gazette* (TTG) regularly to find out more about what is happening in the travel industry. See if your school or college subscribes to TTG. If not, you might be able to find a local travel agent who is willing to pass on past copies.

Task 4

Carry out some independent research or work in pairs to find out about recent (in the last 12 months) mergers and/or acquisitions by integrated tour operators or in other sectors of the travel and tourism industry – for example, hotels, airlines, travel agencies.

As a class, make up a display called 'Merger mania!' to show the dynamic nature of the travel and tourism industry.

RECENT DEVELOPMENTS, TRENDS AND FACTORS SHAPING THE TRAVEL AND TOURISM INDUSTRY

ACTIVITY 3

Since the 1960s, there have been many developments including new destinations, advances in transport and the development of new products, to cater for changing lifestyles.

There have been winners and losers in the development stakes. One of the losers is often seen to be the British seaside resort as can be seen from the following extracts, which can be found in an article entitled 'Every destination has its day – or does it?'

The full article can be found at: http://www.tourismknowledge.com/destinations.htm

The article tracks the demise of the seaside resort of New Brighton in north-west England:

The slow decline of British seaside resorts is well documented and has been the subject of numerous academic studies and subsequent government intervention. It has been common to all British regions, not just in the north west. Whilst the blame usually centres on the explosion of the package holiday market in the 1970s and the outward migration of the UK tourist to European beaches, there were many resorts that suffered market failure much earlier, primarily as a result of private car ownership and the added choice and flexibility it could offer British residents.

New Brighton's heyday was probably in the Edwardian period. It was both a holiday resort with extensive visitor accommodation and a destination for day-trippers. Visitors travelled by rail to Liverpool, took a ferry from the Pier Head and disembarked at Wallasey and New Brighton for a day on the beach. New Brighton boasted some superlatives in its time. The Tower, located near the seafront, was the tallest in Britain and at 621ft was actually 103ft higher than Blackpool's. It was built in 1898 but only survived until 1921 when it was demolished due to structural decay following World War 1.

However, the Tower Ballrooms and entertainment complex survived until 1969. New Brighton also hosted one of the largest open-air swimming pools in the country, a magnificent marine promenade and until the 1960s, featured a miniature steam railway and permanent fairground.

Photographs of New Brighton between the wars continue to show crowded promenades, theatres that could attract top of the bill performers, circuses, fairs and a pier packed to capacity with day-trippers.

Guest houses were fully booked throughout the season. The beaches were as crowded as those of modern day Florida and this continued even until the mid 1960s, although by this time the fading image had now become noticeable.

Gradually, the hotels and bed and breakfast establishments closed or changed use until there were hardly any left. The whole tourism infrastructure began to disintegrate and the spiral of decay accelerated.

New Brighton's decline from the 1970s onwards reflected the general problems of neighbouring Liverpool and Birkenhead with high rates of unemployment, an exodus of employers and industry, the deterioration of the physical fabric of the resort and a complete loss of business confidence.

Bournemouth is then offered for comparison:

The dice were loaded in Bournemouth's favour in several ways: unlike New Brighton, it was not a satellite to a larger city and was not bordered by industrial areas; it enjoyed a warmer climate with very mild winters; it had better natural resources including miles of south facing sandy beaches; the tourism product in terms of hotels, parks and attractions was better developed and much larger.

Another key factor was the point that Bournemouth had established itself with a reputation for quality and could attract a wider range of visitors from families on a budget to the internationally select who were seeking five-star luxury.

At the same time, Bournemouth still had to tackle the common problems facing all seaside destinations. The traditional summer holiday was being replaced by shorter visitor stays. The demand for serviced accommodation was reducing. It suffered the pressures of an ageing population and related demand for changes of use from hotels to rest homes. For many years the Council was indecisive in terms of destination planning issues – a debate about a local marina floated around for at least three decades – and big capital projects always took years of debate and argument.

Several factors helped rescue the town from the downward slope that faced some of its competitors. It had begun to diversify from the traditional market. For example, a flourishing language school sector had extended the number of overseas visitors staying with local families, providing much-needed secondary spending and employment opportunities, especially in the off-peak and shoulder seasons. After many delays, the town finally agreed to build a conference centre that could compete with Blackpool and Brighton for both conference and exhibition delegates.

The Council continued to invest in tourism infrastructure such as rebuilding the pier and whilst many facilities were already owned in-house it began to contract out areas such as bars, beach services and catering.

In the meantime, the quality image of the location helped secure wider inward investment with the town attracting many new tertiary industries, particularly insurance and financial service companies, thus relieving the pressure of having a single-industry employer. The upgrading of the higher education establishment to a university and a big influx of students has also helped rid Bournemouth of its image of 'God's Waiting Room', so that the town feels more youthful and establishments catering for younger people can be sustained all year round.

The conference centre no doubt saved many large and medium-sized hotels from closure and has resulted in greater off-peak usage of accommodation. Whilst there has been some homogenisation of hotel stock gravitating both upward and downward to middle-range three-star, the accommodation on offer still remains varied providing a wide choice to business and leisure users. Together with a well-managed summer programme of events, much of it family orientated, and an acceptance that many visitors are using the resort as a secondary holiday destination, Bournemouth has been able to redevelop its image without having to completely re-draft its tourism product. The town's greatest assets, its town centre parks and beaches, remain the key driver of the brand image.

Task 1

Produce two lists, one giving reasons for the demise of UK seaside destinations and the other showing how destinations like Bournemouth have been able to succeed where other resorts have failed.

Compare your list with a colleague's, noting any omissions.

Task 2

As a class, discuss and agree the main reasons why Bournemouth has developed into a successful destination today.

Task 3

Carry out research to find evidence of current trends, for example:

- Increased frequency of holidays
- More independent travellers
- Growth and expansion of regional airports
- Greater flexibility of booking and products.

Can you find evidence of other trends?

Examine ways in which destinations like Bournemouth could continue to develop in response to current trends.

Working in pairs, put your ideas on a poster entitled 'Bournemouth: The future!'

ACTIVITY 4

Here is an extract from an article in the 26 May 2007 edition of the *Daily Express*, showing how products and services have been developed to cater for changing consumer demands:

Hello Cool Campers

Alex Bailey, 27, and his 26-year-old girlfriend Louise Vernon live in London's uber-cool Islington and are discerning twentysomethings. She's a marketing manager, he's a lawyer in the City and they spend their evenings attending gigs and eating in gastropubs with friends. They are also ardent travellers.

So far this year they have jetted off for a fortnight in St Lucia, enjoyed four nights on the spectacular Cornish Coast, booked their tickets for a weekend in Barcelona for a friend's wedding – and spent three nights at Butlins in sunny Bognor Regis on the south coast.

Err, that's right – Butlins, but not perhaps as you imagine it. If you conjure up a time warp of knobbly knees competitions, glamorous granny parades and brightly painted wooden chalets then think again. The holiday camp has undergone a renaissance and that applies to the other chains as well. Pontins and Haven have had to diversify and modernise to survive, while Warners now offers holidays for adults only.

...Today the 71-year-old Butlins brand has been reinvigorated beyond recognition thanks to the £250 million that has been pumped into it by the new owners over the past seven years.

It is now possible to get a Hawaiian massage using Lomi Lomi techniques at the Butlins Skegness Spa, cut a CD, perform live with a seven-piece band, learn to dive, go on a Land Rover safari, brush up your DJ skills, have some professional football coaching or try out the aerial ropes.

At Pontins' eight resorts you can go quad biking, learn circus skills or do rifle shooting. Meanwhile some of Haven's 34 holiday parks are offering salsa weekends and grand-slam wrestling this summer.

47

Task 1

Carry out further research into Butlins and produce a time line to chart how the product has developed to cater for lifestyle changes and changing consumer demand over the years.

Task 2

Examine the current Butlins product from the perspective of three different markets: 'young twentysomethings', families and the over 50s.

Identify new products and services that have been developed for each of these markets. Explain how these new products or services will appeal to the age groups listed above.

Task 3

Center Parcs offer a completely different type of holiday centre. Carry out some research into Center Parcs in the UK.

In small groups discuss how environmental factors and lifestyle changes may have had an impact on the past and current development of Center Parcs in the UK. Compare your findings with other groups.

ACTIVITY 5

Even the Spanish resorts that wooed the British holidaymaker away from the traditional seaside and holiday camps in the 1960s and 1970s have found themselves suffering as a consequence of changing consumer demands, new destinations and lifestyle changes.

According to a story featured by BBC news on 7 April 2007, Spanish resorts no longer hold the same appeal for UK visitors.

Some extracts are presented below:

> It's the end of the 50-year holiday romance. Decades of over-development have led to some of Spain's most popular resorts falling from favour with British tourists. Yet it was the Costa Brava which first sparked our enthusiasm for taking trips abroad.
>
> The Costa Brava of 50 years ago sounds just the ticket for today's holidaymaker, who seeks sun, sand, sea and seclusion on a seemingly undiscovered beach.
>
> The first package tour touched down in 1954, when the Catalan coast was populated not by high-rise hotels but clusters of quaint fishing villages.
>
> Today it is one of many striving to shake off the image of a cheap-as-chips concrete jungle – some, such as the Balearic island of Mallorca, with more success than others.
>
> Today, with bookings down almost a quarter on the same time last year, tour company First Choice has dropped the region from its summer brochure.
>
> Other tour operators have expressed doubts about the region, among them Club 18-30, which began in 1965 when it took 580 fun-seekers to the Costa Brava. The company – which has a reputation for encouraging drinking and bawdiness among its clientele – has now pulled out of Lloret de Mar and Benidorm on the grounds that the resorts are not 'sophisticated' enough.
>
> *http://news.bbc.co.uk/go/pr/fr/-/2/hi/uk_news/magazine/3604007.stm*

48

Task 1

If Club 18-30 has pulled out of Lloret de Mar and Benidorm on the grounds that they are not sophisticated enough, find out which new 'sophisticated' destinations have taken their place. What do these new resorts offer 18–30-year-olds?

Examine the Club 18-30 brochures to see if it has dropped its wild drinking reputation. What evidence is there to support your view?

Task 2

The article suggests that Mallorca has had more success than other Spanish destinations at shaking off its cheap image. Carry out research to find out how Mallorca has achieved this.

In what ways has Mallorca responded to changing trends?

How could Mallorca continue to develop in the future to cater for changing trends?

Task 3

Divide into groups to discuss the reasons for the decline of some package holidays.

Consider how developments such as the Internet and low-cost airlines have affected the popularity of package holidays.

Identify ways in which tour operators have responded, or could respond, to these issues.

Discuss your findings with other groups.

ACTIVITY 6

Travel and tourism providers must constantly look at developing new products to meet consumer demand. The variety offered by airlines is enormous, not just in terms of destinations served, but also in terms of the products and services they offer, from budget no-frills to luxury first class.

It seems that there is no limit to the efforts of the travel and tourism industry to jump on the bandwagon and embrace new consumer trends, as is seen in the following extracts from a newspaper article in the *Sunday Express* on 27 May 2007:

I'm just nipping to the shops, love. Do you have any Euros?

The WAGS have been doing it for years – but now every woman's dream is about to come true with the launch of an airline for shopping trips to Paris, Milan and New York. Called FlyPink in homage to all things girly, the airline which promises to put the glamour back into air travel, has a totally frivolous fuschia-pink livery. It makes its inaugural flight to Paris next month from Liverpool's John Lennon Airport.

Passengers will sip pink champagne in a pink themed cabin aboard the 100-seat Fokker aircraft. They will even be treated to a free manicure at the airport before they fly. The boutique airline is aimed at Coleen McLoughlin and Victoria Beckham wannabes aged 21–35. Fares, which include 'gourmet' food and drink will be between £140 and £170.

… FlyPink will be as different as possible to budget airlines such as Ryanair. The airline is also intended to be 'carbon-neutral' – a tree will be planted for every passenger to offset carbon emissions.

… FlyPink chose Liverpool because it is one of the fastest growing airports in the UK with 5.6 million passengers a year and should attract many tourists next year as the European Capital of Culture.

… The girly concept has already proved a hit with 5000 women surveyed in the Liverpool area, close to the WAGS' stomping ground in Cheshire.

Task 1

Liverpool John Lennon Airport is already well served by scheduled, charter and low-cost scheduled airlines. Find out which airlines already fly from Liverpool to the three destinations mentioned in the extract.

Task 2

Compare the timings, cost and product offered by FlyPink, one low-cost airline and one regular scheduled airline.

From your findings, discuss how successful you think FlyPink will be.

Task 3

Whatever next? Carry out research to find out about recent aviation initiatives – for example, business-only flights to New York.

As a class, discuss how the aviation industry might continue to develop its products and services in the future.

ACTIVITY 7

According to online travel provider Opodo, the top three travel destinations for 2007 were forecasted to be Bulgaria, Russia and Morocco:

2006 has seen a strong rise in travel to Eastern European countries since whilst being accessible, they still hold a certain 'mystique' for the traveller. Bookings to Bulgaria have risen by 40% in the last 6 months and with the prospect of joining the EU in January '07, we expect to see a significant increase in the number of tourists heading there to take advantage of the euro. Russia will also continue to grow in popularity for those looking for their next Eastern European adventure, an insight which is apparent from the 24% increase in bookings so far this year.

Morocco will also become one of the biggest tourist hotspots of 2007, with so many beautiful and affordable boutique-style hotels springing up. Flight prices have dropped dramatically and the country is much more accessible than before. It's a reasonably short flight and the country is so vastly different that tourists can quickly immerse themselves in another culture, something that is very appealing in this day and age. The stunning hotels and diverse people, combined with general easier access, mean that the country is now appealing to the cash rich and time poor.

http://www.opodo.co.uk/opodo/StrutsServlet/DisplayNewsStory?page Name=pressroom&OID=32690

Task 1

The emergence of new short-haul destinations has been largely attributed to the recent rise in regional airports and low-cost carriers.

Carry out some research to see if the three destinations are served by regional airports and low-cost carriers.

To what extent do you think these two factors have contributed to the increase in visitors to these three destinations? Discuss as a class.

Task 2

Identify other developments and factors that have contributed to the appeal of these destinations.

Task 3

It is now easier than ever to use the Internet to make independent travel arrangements to destinations such as Bulgaria, Russia and Morocco.

Can you find evidence that tour operators have responded to the increased demand for more flexible and independent holidays?

ACTIVITY 8

Tour operators must constantly expand and develop their product ranges to cope with changing consumer demand. One area of increased demand is for getting married overseas.

In the January 2007 TTG supplement 'Weddings and Honeymoons' it was reported:

- In 2006 the average cost of a wedding was £17,000 according to Mintel. Marrying abroad is almost six times cheaper.

- As well as being less expensive, 80% of couples think that organising a wedding abroad is less stressful, with the most popular reason for escaping these shores being to avoid family feuds.

Task 1

You can now take your wedding vows in many countries around the world and this has become big business for a number of tour operators.

In small groups, select a tour operator offering a 'Weddings and Honeymoons' programme, making sure that there is no repetition within the class.

Using a large wall map, plot your company's wedding destinations (you could use company logos to do this).

From the number of entries on the map, work out the 'Top Ten' wedding destinations featured in the brochures.

Task 2

It's not plain sailing being a wedding organiser. In pairs, select one overseas destination and find out what the requirements are for a couple from the UK to get married in that country.

Task 3

Divide into small groups, each taking one of the following 'alternative' weddings:
- An Arctic wedding
- A bungee wedding
- A safari wedding
- A Disneyland wedding
- An underwater wedding
- A themed wedding (eg Elvis Presley, Roman gladiators).

51

Research your chosen theme and find at least one example of:

- A tour operator featuring this kind of wedding
- A destination where you can 'tie the knot' in this way
- A typical 'package' available for this wedding.

Produce a class display containing details of all the wacky and wonderful weddings that you have found.

ACTIVITY 9

Note down which of the following 'trends' you have found in the articles in this section:

- Increased frequency of holidays
- Greater flexibility (of booking, of products)
- More independent travellers
- Adventure travel
- New destinations
- Growth and expansion of regional airports
- Secondary holidays.

This list is not exhaustive. Can you identify any other trends?

ACTIVITY 10

Environmental issues have become topical in recent years and many travel and tourism organisations have re-assessed their products, services, business practices and values in the light of growing concerns about the impacts on the environment.

There are many terms used to describe this growing trend:

> Sustainable tourism, eco-tourism, Green tourism. There are many labels, but whatever you prefer to call it, the definition remains the same: low impact, environmentally-friendly tourism that cherishes, not destroys.
>
> As a market strategy, sustainable Green tourism makes eminent sense for the long term, and taps into what is a growing demand for holidays that leave the smallest possible 'footprint' on the environment and local communities.
>
> *http://www.hie.co.uk/tourism/green-tourism.htmltask*

Task 1

What do you think is meant by 'smallest possible "footprint"' in this quote?

As a class, discuss ways in which travel and tourism organisations could avoid leaving a large footprint on the environment and local communities.

Task 2

Take a look at this picture:

As a class, discuss what you think are the responsibilities of travel and tourism organisations to local people like this.

Task 3

Imagine that you are a tour operator introducing holidays to a new destination, an unspoiled island in the Indian Ocean.

As a class, discuss ways in which a tour operator could threaten the way of life of the indigenous population.

As a class, discuss ways in which a tour operator could protect and enhance the way of life of the indigenous population.

With a partner, design two posters: one to show the positive impacts and the other to show the negative impacts of tourism for the indigenous population.

Task 4

In this task you will carry out some research into one of the large tour operators – for example, Thomas Cook, Thomson Holidays, First Choice – and find out how they are responding to the growing awareness of environmental issues and the growing interest in responsible tourism.

As a class, divide into four groups, each researching a different tour operator, and present your findings to the rest of the class. Produce a display to support your findings.

Discuss which tour operator you feel is taking the most proactive role in dealing with environmental issues.

Can you suggest anything else tour operators could do to respond to environmental issues?

Task 5

Something to think about …

> While those of us fortunate enough to be able to afford the luxury of foreign travel agonise over our carbon footprints, the livelihoods of people in developing countries, where tourism is often the backbone of the economy, are also hanging in the balance.
>
> *Joanne O'Connor The Guardian:*
>
> *http://www.justtheflight.co.uk/features/5-fly-your-way-to-eco-friendliness.html*

What does this mean? What evidence can you find to support this comment?

ACTIVITY 11

The aviation industry has received much criticism for the damage it inflicts on the environment.

The following article can be found at: http://www.justtheflight.co.uk/features/5-fly-your-way-to-eco-friendliness.html

With climate change being the hot topic of the moment (and for many years to come, no doubt), travellers might be wondering how they can help to fight the murky spectre of rising carbon emissions. Happily, there are a number of ways in which holidaymakers can minimise their emissions and do their bit for the environment.

Where to begin?

Firstly, how does travel affect the environment? Pretty much every form of petrol-powered motor travel – cars, buses, planes – releases emissions that contain carbon dioxide and other harmful gases.

These carbon emissions, if left unchecked, can build up in the planet's atmosphere and absorb more of the sun's rays than they should. This contributes towards global warming, where temperatures across the world rise and can result in higher sea levels and changes in rainfall patterns.

However, despite all the media attention currently focused on flights and their carbon emissions, research from a number of sources has indicated that aircraft account for a relatively small fraction of the UK's total carbon output.

In spite of this, holidaymakers should still attempt to be as green as possible – as every little counts.

Get planting

One way of reducing the harm caused to the planet by holiday flights is to make up for the amount of carbon you contribute through a carbon offsetting scheme. Through websites such as Treeflights, all you have to do is calculate how much carbon dioxide your flight will emit and pay for trees to be specially planted in order to counter your emissions.

The cost and the number of trees will vary depending on how long your flight is, but £10 could be enough to offset a journey between London and New York.

Green Airlines?

There's also the question of whether it's possible to board a flight that is in itself eco-friendly. Increasing numbers of airlines are waking up to the green issue and are implementing initiatives to help ease passengers' consciences.

Last October, British Airways announced that it was looking into upgrading some of its fleet to more environmentally-friendly models. Spanish airline Iberia has also set out its green credentials with a scheme devised to draw passengers' attentions to the plight of protected and endangered species through paintings on newly-acquired aircraft.

In addition, research is ongoing into the possible use of biofuels, which are renewable because they are based on organic sources like palm oil and even manure. While you won't be able to set foot on a biofuel-powered plane in the near future, it's possible that scientists will eventually come up with a way of making flights that little bit greener.

Task 1

With a partner, carry out research to see if you can find any evidence to support the claim that 'aircraft account for a relatively small fraction of the UK's total carbon output'.

Through your research, see if you can find evidence of any other types of transport used in travel and tourism that might bear a greater responsibility for carbon emissions.

Share your findings with the rest of the class.

Task 2

Carry out research to find out more about what airlines are doing to minimise their impact on the environment.

As a class, research a wide range of airlines, including scheduled, low-cost scheduled and charter airlines to find out if they are making changes to their products and services to protect the environment.

During your research, see if you can find examples of any airlines that are using the 'green' agenda as part of their marketing strategy – for example, in their advertisements.

Discuss your findings and decide on the 'Top Ten' airlines, based on their efforts to become more environmentally-friendly.

Task 3

Have you flown as part of a holiday within the past 12 months?

If so, go to http://www.chooseclimate.org/flying/mf.html to find out the environmental impact of your flight.

Organisations like Treeflights allow you to purchase a tree for £10 to help offset the environmental impact of your flight.

As a class, discuss whether initiatives such as this have any real impact on our travel decisions.

While the sentiment might be something to applaud, would it not be better for us to just limit our air travel? Think about how you would feel if you usually travel by air on holiday and this was restricted. Would you be prepared to stay in the UK or travel by other means?

Find out what the general consensus is in the class.

ACTIVITY 12

Global warming is said to be threatening our wildlife.

Task 1

Find examples of organisations that have been developed in response to the growing demand for more responsible tourism.

In groups, discuss and recommend ways in which travel and tourism organisations could do more to respond to environmental issues.

Task 2

On your own, design a questionnaire to find out whether people would be prepared to pay more or change the way that they travel for holidays or for business in order to minimise the impact on the environment.

As a class, compare your designs and agree on a final version. If each member of the class is able to use the questionnaire to carry out research with at least ten people, you could have a reasonable-sized sample for analysis. Don't forget it would be useful to find out something about their age, occupation and their usual business or holiday travel patterns.

Analyse the responses. This means that you should study all of the information carefully and make your own conclusions. Then discuss ways in which the travel and tourism industry might respond.

This unit focuses on grading criteria P4, M2 and D1.

Unit overview

This section considers the needs of UK and domestic and inbound tourism markets and the ways in which the UK meets those needs.

The UK has something for everyone, from its beautiful scenery to cosmopolitan cities; from picturesque villages to bustling resorts. The challenge of the UK travel and tourism industry is to meet the needs of many different types of visitor. This section will introduce you to some of the many differing needs of the inbound and domestic tourism markets.

If you have the opportunity to travel in the UK while you are taking this qualification, take note of what different destinations have to offer. If you are fortunate enough to live near a well-known tourist destination, try to look at it through the eyes of different types of visitor. You might be surprised at what you find!

Learning outcomes

4 Understand the needs of UK domestic and inbound tourism markets and the ways in which the UK meets those needs

Content

4) **Understand the needs of UK domestic and inbound tourism markets and the ways in which the UK meets those needs**

Definitions: domestic tourism; inbound tourism

Domestic tourism markets: eg schools, families, businesses, honeymoons, groups

Domestic tourist needs: access to information, eg brochures, internet; accommodation; transport (within destination, to destination); facilities, eg for families, for older people, special events; attractions; leisure activities; experience something new

Inbound tourism markets: businesses; leisure, eg short break, special interest

Inbound tourist needs: local and national customs and traditions; special events; attractions, eg heritage, culture; accommodation preferences; transport, eg car hire, ferries, international airports and services; quality assurance; novelty; access to information, eg brochures, internet.

Grading criteria

P4 describe the needs of the UK domestic and inbound tourism markets

You will need to demonstrate that you have a good understanding of the needs of one type of domestic tourist (for example, a honeymoon couple), the inbound business tourist and the inbound leisure tourist. You will need to cover all of the needs stated in the Content section.

M2 explain how four specific UK destinations can meet the needs of domestic and inbound tourist markets

This enables you to make a detailed examination of four different destinations and to make judgements about how effectively they meet the needs of different types of domestic and inbound tourist markets. Contrasting destinations will facilitate this examination, so try to include a range of different types of destination in different areas of the UK. It is essential that you explain, rather than describe, how each of the four destinations meets the needs of domestic and inbound tourist markets.

D1 evaluate the attraction of the UK for domestic and inbound markets, making recommendations about how appeal to domestic and inbound tourism can be increased

Expanding on the evidence you have already found, you must now evaluate the attraction of the UK for both inbound and domestic markets. You should make some judgements about how effective you consider the four destinations to be when meeting the needs of these tourists. You will need to consider what their attractions are (including new developments, products and initiatives) and how these could be enhanced to widen appeal to different markets.

INTRODUCTION

UK destinations compete with one another to gain market share. They also face ever-increasing competition from overseas.

From a domestic perspective, British destinations have had to 'fight back' many times; competing against the rise of the package holiday market and the 'Rush to the Sun' in the 1960s and 70s; reacting to changing trends for more exotic locations and culture in the 80s and 90s, and responding to the challenges created by the rise of budget airlines in recent years. With flights to Venice and Gerona for only 1p each way in 2007 (before taxes etc), it is little wonder that many Brits have shunned what Britain has to offer and taken full advantage of these 'giveaway prices'.

On the international stage the UK has to compete with the attraction of exotic destinations and needs to encourage inbound tourists to visit the UK despite unreliable weather, perceptions of poor service and value for money and other factors such as the perceived threat from terrorism.

None the less, the British travel and tourism industry constantly fights back, wooing both domestic and inbound tourists with destination and product development, new initiatives and events and well-targeted marketing.

Here are some facts and figures provided by VisitBritain:

Key Tourism Facts

Tourism is one of the largest industries in the UK, accounting for 3.5% of the UK economy and worth approximately £85 billion in 2005, comprising:

Spending by Overseas Residents	£ billion
Visits to the UK	14.2
Fares to UK carriers	2.8

Spending by Domestic Tourists	£ billion
Trips of 1+ nights	22.7
Day Trips	44.3
Rent for Second Ownership	0.9

Inbound Tourism to the UK:

- The **32.1 million** overseas visitors who came in 2006 spent **£15.4 billion** in the UK. 2006 was a **record year** for UK inbound tourism both in terms of volume and value (in nominal terms)

- Total visits for 2006 are 32.1 million visits, a 7% increase compared with 2005, with an increase of 8% in spending to **£15.4 billion**

- In 2005 the UK ranked fifth in the international tourism earnings league behind the USA, Spain, France and Italy

- The **top five overseas markets** for the UK in 2005 were:

Country	Visits (000)	Country	Spend (£m)
USA	3438	USA	2384
France	3324	Germany	998
Germany	3294	Irish Republic	895
Irish Republic	2806	France	796
Spain	1786	Spain	697

UK Domestic Tourism:

- Expenditure in 2005 is estimated to be over **£68 billion**

- In 2005 UK residents took:

  - **59.3 million** holidays of one night or more spending **£11.5 billion**

  - **22.5 million** overnight business trips spending **£5.3 billion**

  - **52.7 million** overnight trips to friends and relatives spending **£5.4 billion**.

Employment:

- Over 2 million jobs are sustained by tourism activity in the UK, either directly or indirectly

- There are an estimated **1.4 million** jobs directly related to tourism activity in the UK, some **5%** of all people in employment in the UK

- Approximately **130 400** of these jobs are in **self-employment**.

Labour Market Trends: April 2005

	Total (millions)	Tourism-related (millions)
Total Employment	28.4	1.42
Employee Jobs	24.6	1.29
Self-Employment	3.6	0.13

Source: Labour Market Trends April 2005

Accommodation:

- In 2003, the turnover of the hotel industry was **£10.9 billion**. This represented an increase of 4% compared to 2002

- In 2005, average room occupancy for all serviced accommodation throughout the UK was **59%** (down 2 percentage points from 2004). Average bed-space occupancy was **44%** (a decrease of 1 percentage point on 2004).

Source: http://www.tourismtrade.org.uk/MarketIntelligenceResearch/ KeyTourismFacts.asp

It is difficult to grasp the implications of these figures; however, it is clear that tourism is important to the British economy and that both domestic and inbound visitors have a huge part to play in the continued growth of tourism in the UK.

Think again about these statistics:

- In 2005 Britain's second largest market in terms of spend was_____?

- The combined spend of UK domestic holidays, business trips and VFR trips in 2005 was_____?

- The top overseas market in terms of visits and spend in 2005 was _____?

You can see from the statistics that the travel and tourism industry is very important to the UK economy. You will be looking in more detail at the volume and value of inbound and domestic tourism as you progress through Unit 3, so if you come across useful statistics while you are carrying out research into inbound and domestic tourism, make sure that you bookmark the information for your future assignment work.

ACTIVITY 1

Who are the UK's tourists and what are their needs? This is a vast area for research so we will start by looking at the UK domestic tourism market.

It would be too simple to fit the domestic tourist market into neat little boxes. If you did, it might look something like this:

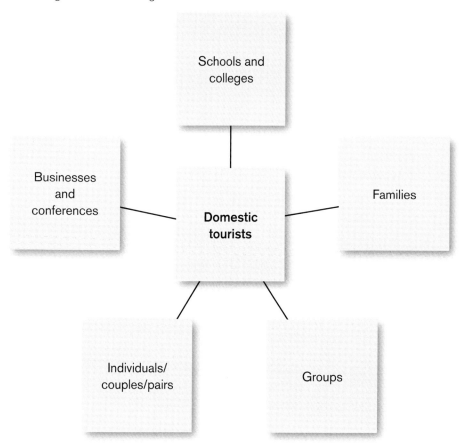

However, this is a very simplistic diagram as there are many variations within these types of domestic tourist, each with differing needs when visiting destinations in the UK.

Let's think about each group in turn.

Schools and colleges. Consider the huge age span of the children and students involved and the types of visits that you might have participated in during your school and/or college years (cultural trips, geography field trips, historical cities, activity trips, days at the coast and so on).

Families. Consider the differing needs of families with babies, toddlers, pre-school, primary-school age, secondary-school age children, extended families … or a combination of some (or even all) of these! What they will be looking for in a destination will differ significantly.

Groups. Again, there is a huge range here. A group could be anything from a group of 'stags' or 'hens', cub scout groups, girl guides, the Women's Institute, groups of gardening enthusiasts, sports groups, music groups. The list is pretty much endless.

Businesses. The domestic business market is extensive – for example, the individual sales manager travelling around the UK, business meetings being held in different locations, training courses for individuals or groups of people, or organisations hosting 1000-delegate business conferences.

Couples/individuals/pairs. This is almost 'everyone else': individuals, couples, friends taking leisure trips or visiting friends and family. Special occasions like an anniversary or honeymoon could be drivers here.

In addition, any of these categories could include or be made up of people with special needs.

From this you can see that it is not a simple thing to look at the 'needs of the domestic tourism market'.

Task 1

As a class, divide into groups, each taking one of the categories listed above and discuss how the needs of tourists within your category might differ. Consider the needs of your category in terms of:

- Access to information
- Accommodation
- Transport
- Facilities
- Events
- Attractions
- Leisure activities.

(For example, families with children of different ages will have differing needs in almost all of these areas.)

Produce a poster to summarise the needs of your selected category.

As a class, discuss the similarities and differences between the categories.

Task 2

Continuing in groups, examine how a local tourist destination meets the needs of your selected category of domestic tourist. When you are carrying out your research, take all the variables for your category into account, eg families of differing ages and interests, different types of groups etc.

Task 3

Make up a class display to show how the local destination meets the needs of different types of domestic tourist.

Task 4

As a class, discuss how well your local destination meets the needs of different categories of domestic visitor. Suggest ways in which it could improve for any of the categories.

ACTIVITY 2

Just as domestic tourists have differing needs, so too do inbound tourists. After all, there will be many different types of visitors within the different nationalities, so many of the points that you have identified relating, for example, to families, will apply also to families coming to the UK from different countries.

When we think of different nationalities we often picture and then talk about certain stereotypes. What nationalities do the following pictures suggest?

Not all stereotypes are accurate. When considering these activities, looking at the needs of different nationalities visiting the UK, we have to look beyond stereotypes. It's useful to identify aspects of visitors' own culture and interests to understand their real needs when visiting the UK.

The VisitBritain website www.visitbritain.co.uk contains intelligence reports containing the results of market research into inbound visitors from different countries.

Task 1

Divide into five groups and carry out research into inbound visitors. Each group should select one of the 'Top Five overseas markets':

- USA
- France
- Germany
- Irish Republic
- Spain.

Find out at least five facts about your selected market that might be of interest to an inbound travel and tourism organisation, for example:

- Age profiles of visitors to the UK
- What motivates them to travel to the UK, eg culture, education, history, nightlife, shopping, visit to friends or relatives, special interests, business
- Average length of stay
- How they travel to the UK
- Who they travel with, ie lone traveller, couple/pair, family group, group of friends, business group, tour group, etc.

Task 2

Make a presentation to the class to share your findings.

Task 3

Discuss similarities between these inbound markets and identify the main features that attract visitors from them to the UK.

ACTIVITY 3

Here is an article about different types of inbound visitor to Scotland:

VisitScotland's award-winning international marketing operation currently costs around £27 million a year. International tourists account for about 14 per cent of total visitors to Scotland, with 86 per cent coming from elsewhere in the UK and Ireland.

With the industry worth about £4.5 billion a year to the economy, we examine what the world's tourists want from Scotland and what the nation can do for them.

SWEDEN

SWEDEN is Scotland's seventh most important tourist market and is worth £48 million a year, thanks to the intense interest of Swedes in the game of golf.

Five per cent of overseas visitors come from Sweden. In 2005 they made 131,000 trips – only just short of the number arriving from Australia.

But unlike some American and Russian tourists, Swedes are happy to enjoy a round anywhere as long as the scenery is good.

'Many visitors from Sweden come through Prestwick to play at Turnberry, but equally a lot of them are happy to play on ordinary municipal courses,' says a spokeswoman for VisitScotland. 'They are just pleased to be playing a round in the country which is the home of golf rather than being hung up about the historical status of the course.'

Swedes are also keen on outdoor and adventure activities, which are increasingly important in mitigating the effects of Scotland's reputation for rain.

'Younger visitors, as well as those who come to Scotland for outdoor activities such as climbing or kayaking, are going to have fun whatever the weather,' says Andrew Deeprose of ferry firm Caledonian MacBrayne. 'The aim of our marketing is to attract visitors year-round.'

RUSSIA

They may be lost in translation, but the works of Robert Burns are still popular with tourists from Russia.

The egalitarian principles of Scotland's bard were taught for decades in schools in the former Soviet country.

'I don't know if anyone would remember the words, but certainly they have heard of him,' says Yulia Vaganova, of the Moscow-based tour operator MITS. Russian visitors are much in demand by VisitScotland, as they are among the biggest spenders.

'Russians will spend far more than most Americans while on holiday in Scotland,' reveals a spokeswoman. But while Russia's emerging middle classes are happy to spend their wealth here, they find the transport a little difficult.

'There are no direct flights, and this pushes up the cost and makes it more difficult to come to Scotland,'

says Dmitry Svarovsky, a manager with Atlas travel in St Petersburg.

CHINA

'CASTLES, whisky and more castles' make Scotland a romantic destination for tourists from the world's fastest-growing market, according to Chinese tour operator Li Wenjun.

China has yet to register among Scotland's key tourism markets, but with easier travel the numbers are set to soar.

One exhibitor attracting Chinese attention yesterday was LA Marine, a firm offering bespoke luxury motorboat tours of the west coast for £2,000 a day – 'the same price as a round of golf for a group of ten at most good courses'.

GERMANY

What makes Germany the second most important overseas tourism market for Scotland?

'There are standard tours but also there are a lot of outdoor activities such as walking, which are very popular in Germany,' explains Sabrina Schlesinger, the head of department with Giessen-based tour firm Behringer Touristik. 'There is an increasing emphasis on the environment and that is important when visitors make choices.'

VisitScotland's new focus on eco-friendly accommodation will help boost the annual spending of German visitors – put at £131 million in 2005.

UNITED STATES

Ancestry is still the biggest reason why Americans choose Scotland over other old-world European countries, and the United States is still Scotland's biggest overseas market.

US visitors spent £195 million in Scotland in 2005, accounting for almost £1 in every £5 spent during the year and 14 per cent of all visits from overseas.

But will there be a downturn as the pound continues to strengthen against the dollar?

'That is certainly becoming an issue,' admits Susan Smith, an economic development manager for East Lothian Council, whose area includes some of the world's best golf courses. 'But a lot of the travel is already booked in for this year so the recent changes haven't had any impact yet.'

And while Scotland may be more expensive than southern European countries, it is a bargain compared to parts of Scandinavia.

'We also offer tours to Iceland and Greenland, so Scotland seems cheap, relative to those destinations,' says Michelle Vanrobaeys, a travel consultant with Winnipeg-based Great Canadian Travel. 'The majority of interest in Scotland comes from those with family connections'.

http://thescotsman.scotsman.com/index.cfm?id=601272007

Task 1

From the article, identify eight aspects of Scotland's appeal and also three negative factors that are mentioned. Compare your list with that of a colleague.

Task 2

Find out if anyone in your class has visited Scotland. Which destinations did they visit and what appealed to them most?

Task 3

In October 2006 Edinburgh was named the favourite UK city in the *Guardian* Travel awards for a seventh consecutive year.

There was considerable delight when the *Guardian* newspaper announced that Edinburgh was the UK's favourite city – for the seventh time! The web site www.edinburghbrand.com reported the comments of two of the city's leading advocates. Counsellor Donald Anderson, Executive Member for Sport, Culture and Tourism, said: 'It is a great honour… it confirms what Edinburgh residents already know – they live in the best city in the UK.' Ailsa Falconer, Project Manager of Edinburgh Inspiring Capital, said 'Winning this award is great news for the city.'

Why the unprecedented success of Edinburgh? Diverse attractions are often cited but people who know the city best often argue that it is its compact nature – so much to see in such a small area – that makes it so popular. The world-renowned Edinburgh festival, with its main offering and 'fringe', attracts millions who all seem to leave with a very positive impression. Whatever the ingredients, there is no doubt that Scotland's capital city had the recipe for success.

Edinburgh is clearly a very successful UK tourist destination. You are now going to look at how well Edinburgh meets the needs of an American visitor.

Profile: The Harvards are 'thirtysomething' Americans from Boston planning their honeymoon. They want this to be a trip to remember, spending 4–5 days in Edinburgh as part of a longer stay in Europe. Mr Harvard has Scottish roots and they hope to gain a real taste of Scotland on their short visit. They like history and 'the arts' as well as the great outdoors.

As a class, discuss the needs of the Harvards in terms of:

- Customs and traditions
- Special events
- Attractions
- Accommodation
- Transport, including international airports and services
- Quality assurance
- Novelty
- Access to information.

Work in small groups to propose a suitable itinerary for the Harvards' visit. Swap itineraries with another group and discuss similarities and differences in what you have proposed.

ACTIVITY 4

In the extract from the *Scotsman* on p. 63, ancestry was identified as one of the motivators for inbound tourists. This is supported by the following extracts taken from an article found at: http://www.visitbritain.com/corporate/presscentre/presscentrebritain/copyrightfreearticles/ancestral.aspx

The fascination with tracing one's ancestors is expanding well beyond the shores of the USA. A recent survey by VisitBritain showed that as many as 50 per cent of potential Australian and New Zealand visitors to Britain would like to research their ancestry as part of their trip. Scotland welcomes more than 250,000 visitors looking into their family history every year.

Ancestral tourism visitors to Britain are much like any other sort, wanting to take in the popular sights, go shopping and sample a range of restaurants and pubs. For these people, however, their trip seems to have a deeper meaning as they also go in search of the little village where their ancestor grew up, or the country graveyard which is the resting place of family members.

Research carried out in spare moments at home takes on a startling reality as the places where kith and kin were born, married or died are sought out, visited and photographed. It is not uncommon for emotions to take over, with visitors shedding a tear or two en route, or at least reporting an enjoyable evening spent in a friendly pub as they recount their investigations to the locals!

Tourist organisations are making life easier by presenting material on websites designed to cater for this type of special interest travel. VisitBritain's www.visitbritain.com/ancestry has teamed up with www.ancestry.co.uk to provide a customised family name search function on its home page; while www.homecomingwales.com has a useful section on the origin of Welsh surnames (it is a common misconception that anyone from Wales is called Jones). The Scottish site, www.ancestralscotland.com includes a listing of events which may have a specific clan link, such as Highland Games, while www.discoverireland.com taps into the Irish Genealogical Project with its 15 million records dating from the 17th century.

At some point, every family historian is likely to use the services of the National Archives, which holds the records of the UK government from the 11th century to the present. A visit to the Archives' offices, in Kew, West London, is worthwhile in researching ancestors as it is possible to see and handle a wide range of documents, see regularly-changing exhibitions and relax in a bookshop and café. (www.nationalarchives.gov.uk)

Four hundred miles north in Edinburgh, an exciting development is taking place for those researching their Scottish roots. A new Scottish family history centre will create a 'one-stop-shop' for genealogy research in the centre of the capital by bringing together services currently provided separately by several organisations. Called the Scotland's People Centre and expected to open in autumn 2007, it will enable visitors to search records, some 500 years old, trace their family tree and get a glimpse into the richness of Scotland's past. It will include exhibitions, search rooms and retail spaces and be open to everyone. (www.scotlandspeoplehub.gov.uk)

But why is there such a growing interest in ancestral tourism? Perhaps it is something to do with an urge to return to our roots; a human homing instinct. In the words of Deirdre Livingstone, head of Project Jamestown at VisitBritain: 'People want to see, touch and feel their past. To find and actually touch the gravestones of your ancestors is a powerful thing.'

Task 1

The US, Australian and New Zealand markets are mentioned in the article. Carry out some research into the Australian market to identify other interests when travelling to the UK for leisure purposes.

ACTIVITY 5

The UK must strive to keep up with the needs of new and emerging markets. According to the following extract from a press release on 7 May 2007, the Indian market is growing rapidly:

> Indian visitors to London spent more than Japanese tourists for the first time last year – underlining the scale of the emerging Indian middle class and the strength of the Indian economy.
>
> Figures from VisitLondon show that tourists from India spent £139m last year – up from £107m a year earlier and £78m in 2003. About 212,000 Indians visited London last year, up from 130,000 in 2003.
>
> *Source: http://business.guardian.co.uk/story/0,,2073864,00.html#article_*

A further press release from VisitBritain gives some indication of how the industry is capitalising on the growing interest in 'Bollywood':

AN INDIAN SUMMER

27 May 2007

Britain is gearing up for its own Indian summer with the launch of a new Bollywood Britain map and website, www.visitbritain.com/bollywood. The campaign encourages Indian visitors to follow in the footsteps of their favourite stars and experience the destinations featured in contemporary and classic Bollywood films from the last 20 years.

30,000 maps will be distributed in India to take advantage of the 25% increase in visits last year, which now means that Indians make more visits to the UK than the Japanese. With 40% of potential visitors 'very likely' to visit places from films or TV, VisitBritain expects the appearance of British locations in Bollywood films to help encourage many more visitors. As well as film locations, the Bollywood Britain map highlights the appeal of shopping, food and drink, sport and British culture – all popular attractions and activities for Indian visitors.

Renowned Indian director Yash Chopra says: 'Britain has always been a home away from home. I have shot a lot of my films in Britain and my crew and I have been touched by the warmth of the people and all my shootings there have been memorable. I would love to shoot more and more films in Britain.'

Thirty Bollywood films feature on the map:

- London remains a popular choice and features in *Salaam-E-Ishq* starring Anil Kapoor as well as *Namastey London* with Jason Connery and *Jhoom Barabar Jhoom*, all released for 2007.
- Chelsea Football Club is also a popular draw – and not just because of its international profile. Stamford Bridge hosts the annual Asian Community Cup Final and has hosted celebrity fans Abishek Bachchan, Aishwarya Rai, Preity Zinta and Lara Dutta.
- Elsewhere, England is also proving a popular choice with Indian movies filmed around Bath, Blackpool, Lancaster and Preston, Herefordshire, Hertfordshire, the Lake District, Oxford and Weymouth. Film-makers have also used iconic attractions such as Blenheim Palace, Cliveden

House, Longleat House, Cheshire's Nunsmere Hall, Stowe Gardens in Buckinghamshire, Waddeston Manor and Shropshire's Walcot Hall.

- *Kasam Se* (2001) filmed in Caernarfon and Conwy, while *Kaun Hai Jo Sapno Main Aaya* (2004) shot on location around Caerphilly. Wales has seen visits from India increase by 175% and Indian visitors now spend £10 million in the country, an increase of 233% compared to 2005.

- Indians spent £24 million in Scotland last year, perhaps inspired by the filming of *Pyaar Ishq Aur Mohabbat* (2001) around Edinburgh, Glasgow, Stirling and throughout Scotland, as well as *Kyun…! Ho Gaya Na* (2004) and *Kuch Kuch Hota Hai* (1998).

Tom Wright, chief executive of national tourism agency VisitBritain, says: 'Britain has become the popular choice for the world's biggest movie industry – and VisitBritain has led the way since 1996 in capitalising on this "screen magic"'.

'Some 23 million Indians go to see a film every day and you only have to look at the figures to see that more and more of them are being inspired to visit Britain. Britain's popularity as a Bollywood backdrop can only help us raise our profile among this growing audience and Bollywood Britain will show them all they can enjoy while they are here.'

Following the unveiling of a Madame Tussauds waxwork of Bollywood 'A-lister', Shah Rukh Khan, 2007 is set to be an Indian summer for Britain. The campaign times perfectly with the build up of The International Indian Film Academy (IIFA) Awards taking place from the 7–10 June 2007 in Yorkshire. Dubbed the 'Bollywood Oscars', the IIFA Awards will showcase Yorkshire to a global audience of 315 million.

Then, from July, London stages India Now, a three-month season celebrating Indian culture and culminating in an India-themed Regent Street Festival. India will also be the theme of August's annual cultural arts festival in Trafalgar Square. The summer closes with the much-anticipated release of *The Golden Age*, the sequel to *Elizabeth*, both from Indian director Shekhar Kapur.

India is already one of the fastest growing sources of international visitors for Britain's £85 billion visitor economy. The 339,000 visits made by Indians in 2006 contributed £294 million to the UK's economy – up 25% and 30% respectively compared to 2005 and a new record. VisitBritain has a dedicated film tourism office in Mumbai to explore and develop opportunities and work with major distributors, studios and new film releases.

The importance of India to British tourism

- Between 1993 and 2006 the number of inbound visits and spending from India have risen by 173.4% and 332.4% respectively.

- Business remains the biggest reason for Indians to come to Britain with a 35% share of visits compared to holidays which has a 25% share.

- However, holiday visits are growing much more quickly, rising 35% compared to 2005. Business visits rose 29%.

- Holiday visits and spending by Indians have risen 34.9% and 44.4% respectively compared to 2005, while business visits and spending have increased by 28.6% and 42.3% respectively.

- Holiday visits of 4–7 nights have risen by 66.7% compared to 2005, by far the largest increase in terms of length of stay. In fact, spending on holiday visits of 1–7 nights has risen by 57% and now stands at £22 million. Longer holidays have also increased by 37% to 37,000 visits.

- The 2.6 million visits to Hindi films in the UK last year made them the most popular foreign language film; with Indian films accounting for 16% of all UK releases in total, taking £12.4 million at the UK box office.

Source: http://www.visitbritain.com/corporate/presscentre/presscentrebritain/ pressreleasesoverseasmrkt/jan-apr2007/bollywood.aspx

Task 1

Many UK destinations have increased their appeal to both domestic and inbound markets as a result of films, TV series and literary links.

As a class, carry out some research to identify UK destinations that have benefited from such links.

Task 2

Plot the destinations on a large scale map of the UK.

ACTIVITY 6

Since the UK was awarded Authorised Destination Status (ADS) for the Chinese market in 2005, there has been a significant increase in the volume of Chinese visitors to the UK.

Task 1

This is a photograph of one of the first groups of Chinese visitors arriving in the UK.

What do you think their expectations of Britain might have been when they were setting off from China? Share your ideas as a class, then read the following press release, which was issued in 2005:

Chinese tourists flock to UK in search of Clarks, fog and the 'big stupid clock'.

Britain braced for influx from Beijing after visa rules relaxed

Richard Jinman and Hsiao-Hung Pai
Monday June 27, 2005

The Chinese were well-prepared. Armed with paper cutouts of their relatives' feet, they leaped from their coaches and headed straight for the racks of shoes at the Clarks shop. 'It was a bit of a frenzy,' said a staff member at Bicester Village, a collection of factory outlets near Oxford visited by a group of 2,000 Chinese salespeople this month. They bought up to six pairs of shoes each and the queue stretched out of the door.'

Tourism chiefs hope the scenes are a taste of things to come. They are predicting a significant increase in the number of visitors from China following Beijing's decision in January to add the UK to its authorised destination status (ADS) list. In the past, only Chinese businesspeople and students could obtain visas to travel here. From July, an ADS visa will be available that allows groups of five or more Chinese tourists to visit Britain.

The introduction of the visa and the booming Chinese economy is being acknowledged with an increase in the number of flights from China's main cities. British Airways this month launched a Shanghai–London route and increased the number of flights from Beijing.

The first official group of ADS visitors – a party of 80 tourists and VIPs – arrives in the UK on July 24. VisitBritain, the agency organising the trip, believes the new visa will increase the number of annual visits from 96,000 last year to more than 200,000 in 2010. By then, inbound tourism from China will be worth more than £200m and by 2020 China could be among the UK's top ten inbound tourism markets.

Carl Walsh, VisitBritain's overseas markets manager, describes the advent of the ADS visa as 'a huge opportunity'.

'A lot of people are comparing it to when the Japanese first started coming 15 to 20 years ago.'

But what do the Chinese expect to find when they get here? And what will they want to see and do besides emptying the shelves at Clarks factory outlets?

According to Calum MacLeod, director of the Great Britain-China Centre, many Chinese still have an outdated view of Britain shaped by classic literature and old movies.

'Oliver Twist is a very popular book in China and the title of the Chinese version translates as Foggy City Orphan,' he said. 'When I tell people I live in London they often ask me how bad the fog is.' MacLeod says phrases such as 'the home of the industrial revolution' or 'the empire on which the sun will never set' still resonate strongly with many Chinese. 'But not in a particularly negative way,' he said. 'They are very interested in the UK's history and traditions.'

Lai Gaik Ung Polain, a blue badge guide who regularly escorts Chinese groups around the UK, agrees. As well as much-visited attractions such as Buckingham Palace and the Houses of Parliament, Ms Polain says many of her Chinese visitors want to see Blenheim Palace – because Winston Churchill was born there – and the British Museum, because some of them suspect it may contain artefacts stolen from China in the colonial era.

Often, a photograph taken outside an attraction is as good as a visit inside. 'They have to show pictures back home to prove they were there,' Ms Polain said.

According to one current Chinese-language guidebook to Britain, Trafalgar Square, Karl Marx's grave and the British Museum are among the highlights. Westminster's Big Ben clock – Da Ben Zhong in Chinese, which translated directly means 'big stupid clock' – is also praised. 'The most precise time-teller in the UK! Although it did break twice.'

Soho provides a taste of home – 'All Chinese tourists will be taken here because they simply need to eat Chinese food when they are abroad,' says the guide. But that part of London also provides other attractions. 'The male tourists always ask to see the red light district, so they are always taken there. The red light district is not as developed in Britain as in other parts of Europe,' the book says.

The British Museum is a less straightforward attraction. 'The Chinese section contains precious exhibits from the imperial times, many of them given to the British as gifts from the royals. Many feel that these are looted from China.'

Charlie Li, VisitBritain's Beijing representative, insists that old-fashioned perceptions of the UK are fading. Initiatives such as Think Britain – a 2003 scheme designed to educate Chinese people aged 16–35 about contemporary Britain – are having an effect.

'People are realising London is a vibrant, international city and they want to visit,' Ms Li said. 'British people are regarded as kind, gentle, welcoming and civilised.'

Shopping is as important as sightseeing to many Chinese tourists. They are on tight schedules – many will spend only a few days in the UK before moving on to another European country – and they like to buy presents for family, friends and workmates. 'If they have the money, they can go really crazy,' said Ms Polain.

Clarks shoes has a reputation as a prestige brand because it was introduced to China in the 1980s via Hong Kong. Provenance is important to the Chinese when it comes to buying goods, so they are also drawn to brands such as Dunhill and Burberry, which are seen as quintessentially British. Some of these goods may be manufactured in China, but that is not particularly important. 'There is the perception that they are less likely to buy counterfeit goods here,' said Mr MacLeod. 'China is plagued by fake goods and there is a real cachet in having bought something from its place of origin.'

Chinese tourism may have enormous potential, but not everyone believes Britain is doing enough to stimulate a boom. Mr MacLeod, who already brings groups of Chinese professionals to the UK, says not enough hotels, tour operators and attractions are gearing up to meet the specific needs of Chinese tourists. More Chinese signage, brochures and guides need to be created and more hotels should consider offering Chinese newspapers and television as well as Chinese breakfasts.

It is a concern echoed by Stephanie Cheng, the managing director of London-based tour company China Holidays. Britain is not a cheap destination and the UK's £50 ADS visa is expensive compared with a £27 Schengen short-stay visa that allows Chinese tourists to visit 15 EU countries. More needs to be done to cater for the Chinese market, or Britain risks losing out to countries such as France and Germany, Ms Cheng says.

VisitBritain's Mr Walsh does not believe the cost of the ADS visa will discourage Chinese visitors. Many tourism companies are already translating brochures and commentaries into Mandarin and hotels are looking at ways to cater for Chinese guests.

'We are not going to see massive growth in the short term,' he said. 'But the potential is enormous.'

http://www.guardian.co.uk/uk_news/story/0,,1515396,00.html

Task 2

Find out about ADS – how has this made travel to the UK easier for Chinese tourists?

Task 3

Carry out some research to find out the frequency of direct flights between China and the UK. Identify the main carriers and gateways, and plot the routes on a map.

In pairs, carry out some research to find out the most popular destinations for Chinese visitors to the UK. Compare your results with your colleagues and decide on the top five destinations for the Chinese market. Is there a link between gateways and the most popular destinations?

Task 4

Many Chinese people like to take coach trips to see as much as they can in a short space of time. Inbound tour operators cater for their needs. Carry out some research into an inbound tour operator such as Evan Evans Tours and find a tour they offer that would be suitable for the Chinese market. (A full listing of inbound tour operators can be found at www.ukinbound.co.uk.)

As a class, compare your tours. Discuss whether you feel these tours will appeal to other nationalities.

Task 5

The article mentions that the Chinese like shopping for brands. As a class, make up a display of logos of brands that you feel are 'quintessentially British'.

Dlaczego warto odwiedzic Brighton?

If you were Polish you would be delighted to see this greeting on Brighton's website. It shows that Brighton is taking the issue of language seriously.

Here is a press statement from VisitBrighton:

VisitBrighton Launch Polish area on Website

Top of Form

A Polish section has been launched on www.visitbrighton.com, as well as winter break offers in a range of key European languages.

Polish visitors flock to Brighton

Research has confirmed that Polish visitors rather like Brighton and suggests they are among the top 5 European countries who visit the city. In fact, according to VisitBritain, visitors from Poland increased by almost 100% last year, making Polish visitors one of the fastest growing visitor sectors in the UK.

VisitBrighton lead the way in Polish tourist information

So it made perfect sense to add a Polish area to the VisitBrighton website, offering Polish city-breakers the chance to find out more about the city in their own language. It's believed that VisitBrighton is one of the few destinations to offer this feature.

Winter break offers have also been added to the foreign language areas of the site to attract visitors during the winter period, a great time to visit Brighton, when visitors have more of the city to themselves. The offers allow people to make an enquiry in their own language at a hotel that speaks their native tongue – another service not widely offered elsewhere on tourism websites.

Foreign language information

www.visitbrighton.com offers foreign language pages in French, German, Spanish, Italian, Dutch and Polish.

http://www.visitbrighton.co.uk/news/944.asp

Task 1

VisitBrighton's website is user-friendly for many different types of inbound and domestic tourist. Spend some time looking at the website www.visitbrighton.com to see how it is being pro-active in targeting different markets.

Task 2

Brighton has much to offer both inbound and domestic visitors. This is how it is described by EnjoyEngland:

> More than the seaside, more than the city, the mix is more than double the fun. Fashionable, funky and loaded with style, Brighton & Hove has everything you could want – a royal palace, elegant Regency architecture, museums with more, laid-back beach life and superb shopping – on the south coast, just 49 minutes from central London.
>
> Don't miss the Royal Pavilion, home of King George IV, and probably the most exotic, extravagant royal palace in Europe. Stroll along the Victorian Pier and the beachfront, where stylish bars and cafés spill out onto the curved paving, jostling for space with surfer shops, giant sculptures, buskers, fresh fish and artists' studios. For shopping, try The Lanes, smart and chic, and the bohemian North Laine, both good for antiques and designer clothes.
>
> There are museums and galleries galore, special events throughout the year from car rallies to carnivals, and England's largest arts festival in May. For nightlife, there's theatre, music, dance and comedy, lively pubs and bars and around 400 restaurants. And there's a great choice of places to stay – ritzy Five-star seafront hotels, jazzy places with Moroccan-style courtyards, minimalist townhouses and traditional B&Bs.
>
> Detailed City Guide to Brighton
>
> Must See and Do
>
> Royal Pavilion, Brighton
> Brighton Pier, Brighton
> Brighton Museum & Art Gallery, Royal Pavilion Gardens, Brighton
> Hove Museum & Art Gallery, Hove
> Brighton Holiday on Ice (January)
> Brighton Sea Life, Brighton
> Preston Manor, Brighton
> Volks Electric Railway, Brighton
> Brighton Fishing Museum, Brighton
> Brighton Marina, Brighton
>
> *http://www.enjoyengland.com/destinations/find/south-east/east-sussex/*
> *brighton.aspx*

In small groups, select a particular segment of the domestic or inbound tourist market and research how effectively Brighton meets the needs of your selected market. As a class, try to cover a range of nationalities and visitor types (eg families, education, older visitors, special needs etc).

Make up a display to show the diverse appeal of Brighton as a destination.

72

ACTIVITY 8

Liverpool as a destination has much to offer both domestic and inbound visitors. The following article, entitled '800 Years Young' was published by VisitBritain in March 2007:

Not content with one, they're celebrating two anniversaries in Liverpool this year. While the 800 years since this maritime city was granted a royal charter by King John in 1207 will be marked with months of merrymaking, the reconstructed Cavern Club, where the Beatles first rose to fame, will enjoy its 50th birthday with a year-long party. Liverpudlians love to party as much as they love football, and the 2007 events will merge neatly into 2008, when the city is again *en fete*, this time as European Capital of Culture.

Some 300 events are organised for this year's 800th anniversary: a veritable feast of concerts, conferences, exhibitions, flower shows, processions, re-enactments, walks and talks. It reaches a peak on August 28, dubbed Liverpool 800 Day, whose festivities climax with one of the world's largest firework displays.

The celebrations couldn't have a better setting architecturally. Liverpool, which rose to prosperity as a trading hub of the British Empire, is filled with grand buildings radiating from its centre to one of Europe's finest river frontages, along the wide River Mersey. UNESCO declared a large swathe of the city, including the river frontage, a World Heritage Site several years ago. With impeccable timing, the neo-classical St. George's Hall – built on an imperial scale complete with statues, a Minton tiled floor and an upstairs concert hall embellished with gold leaf and mirrors – reopens on St. George's Day (April 23) after a £23 million makeover.

Contrasting with these largely Victorian gems are some stunning modern structures, as the city undergoes a 21st-century renaissance. Hotels, apartments, bars, restaurants, stores and new public areas are springing up everywhere. A big development, called the Paradise Project, will provide all these as well as a pleasant walkway linking the city centre and the Albert Docks, where more museums and visitor attractions are located. Biggest development of all is the King's Waterfront, with a new landmark, The Arena and Convention Centre Liverpool, resembling the wings of a giant bird, taking shape on the waterfront. This will be the venue for concerts, exhibitions and conferences from 2008 as well as providing another public piazza.

The city boasts the greatest concentration of National Museums outside London – and admission is free. They are joined by another in August when a £10 million International Slavery Museum opens: Liverpool's role as a lynchpin in the slave trade is something the city is coming to terms with, 200 years after its abolition. Modern art lovers can't fail to be impressed by the Tate Gallery, which occupies a former warehouse in the Albert Docks. The gallery will host the prestigious Turner Prize this autumn – the first time it has been staged outside the capital. The Walker Art Gallery is equally renowned, while the World Museum is filled with hands-on delights for families. The National Maritime Museum is popular, too, not least with thousands of people from overseas, whose ancestors passed through Liverpool as emigrants to a new life. It also houses a new Titanic exhibition: the port was headquarters of the ill-fated ship's White Star Line.

Visitors can stay in any one of a growing number of boutique hotels such as the new Malmaison and the Hope Street Hotel, the last named popular with celebrities and dignitaries such as US Secretary of State Dr. Condoleezza Rice. Next door is the London Carriageworks, one of a growing number of good restaurants which pride themselves in the use of fresh, local produce.

The Cavern Club in Mathew Street sits at the hub of its own quarter of the city, filled with reminders of the 1960s when Beatlemania was at its height, but still turning out great bands, like the Zutons. (Liverpool is listed in the Guinness Book of World Records as having more number one records than any other city.) A highlight of its year is the Mathew Street Festival, when the area is alive with music. The subterranean Cavern – which still manages to evoke the same electric atmosphere as in the heady days of Merseybeat – gets international calls every day from bands that want to come and play on its hallowed stage. These days, Sir Paul McCartney prefers to play in the vast setting of the great Anglican Cathedral – the world's largest – where he premiered his classical *Liverpool Oratorio.*

Climbing to the top of the cathedral tower gives you a breathtaking view of the city and on towards day trip attractions such as the Roman city of Chester with its medieval, galleried shops; a coastline dotted with championship golf courses and, to the east, the bright lights of the city's friendly rival, Manchester.

There is a feeling of youth and vitality everywhere. Students dominate the city centre population, having more than doubled in number in the 1990s and helping fuel the vibrant nightlife, particularly at weekends. Wherever you go – whether it's on board a ferry across the Mersey, on one of the daily tours at Anfield, the home of Liverpool FC, or on the Magical Mystery Tour to the numerous Beatles sights, you are constantly reminded that the people have a great pride in their town. In the words of Peter Smith of Liverpool Vision, 'The people can see the city changing for the better, but our biggest challenge is changing the perceptions of those outside it.'

The Liverpudlians are determined to move their city forward, no longer prepared – in the words of Lennon and McCartney – to simply 'Let It Be'.

*http://www.visitbritain.com/corporate/presscentre/presscentrebritain/
copyrightfreearticles/copyrightfreearticles3/lively_liverpool.aspx*

Task 1

Imagine you are working for VisitLiverpool and you have been asked to review how Liverpool caters for the needs of following types of visitor:

- Domestic Key Stage 3 school groups
- Groups of 'hens' and 'stags'
- Japanese tourists
- American tourists.

Divide into four groups, each taking one of these target groups and identify the needs of your specified group.

Task 2

Carry out detailed research into what Liverpool has to offer each of your visitor types. Consider Liverpool's unique selling points (USPs) and any recent initiatives or new products that have enhanced its appeal.

Task 3

Take part in a class discussion in which you now evaluate the attraction of Liverpool for domestic and inbound visitors and identify gaps in the market and how its appeal could be increased. Consider new developments in the tourism product, transportation and regeneration that might appeal to specific markets.

Task 4

To summarise, produce a poster entitled: 'Liverpool: Our Vision for the future!', with recommendations for how the city's appeal to domestic and inbound tourism could be increased.

UNIT 6 – PREPARING FOR EMPLOYMENT IN THE TRAVEL AND TOURISM INDUSTRY

This unit focuses on grading criteria P1, P2, P5; M1, M3; D1 and D2.

Unit overview

With a wide variety of jobs on offer, the travel and tourism industry is well placed for providing interesting and challenging career opportunities.

In this unit you will investigate a selection of the career options available in different sectors of the travel and tourism industry. The entry requirements, roles and responsibilities for specific jobs will be explored and career progression routes investigated. You will reflect on your own skills, attributes, experience, qualifications and achievements, acknowledging development and training needed to meet specific career aspirations.

Competition for some jobs can be fierce and you will need to be well prepared to create a positive impact during the different stages of recruitment. The unit will introduce you to the typical travel industry recruitment and selection process, examining the different stages from the perspective of both employer and applicant. Personal skills will be developed, enabling you to project yourself positively from the early stages of making job applications through to demonstrating effective interview techniques.

Working practices will be examined to help you to appreciate the factors that motivate employees and contribute to an effective workplace and the importance of a positive working environment.

Learning outcomes

1 Know about career opportunities in the travel and tourism industry

3 Be able to apply for employment in the travel and tourism industry

4 Understand the factors that contribute to an effective workplace

Content

1) Know about career opportunities in the travel and tourism industry

Travel and tourism industry sectors: eg accommodation, transport (rail, road, sea, air), visitor attractions, cruising, tour operations, travel agents, tourism development and promotion, trade associations and regulatory bodies, ancillary services

Jobs: job title; job role; main duties and responsibilities

Entry requirements: qualifications; personal skills and attributes; experience; other factors, eg age, location, Criminal Record Bureau disclosures for working with children

Progression: opportunities for promotion and progression; training; further and higher education

Factors to consider: eg seasonality, temporary, fixed-term contracts, working hours, level of pay, job perks

3) Be able to apply for employment in the travel and tourism industry

Personal skills audit: attributes; skills; experiences; qualifications; achievements

Applying for work: research; CV; application forms (written, online); letters of application; personal statements

Interview skills: advance preparation; company knowledge; telephone screening; attending interviews (individual, group); personal presentation; projecting a positive image; body language; responding to and asking questions; attitude; time management

Evaluation: strengths; weaknesses; areas for improvement

4) Understand the factors that contribute to an effective workplace

Working environment: location; working conditions; hours of work; health and safety; equipment; resources; theorists, eg Maslow, Herzberg; social events; impact on motivation

Working relationships: management style; teamwork, eg Belbin; job roles and lines of responsibility; channels of communication; equal opportunities, eg equal pay, legislative requirements; grievance and disciplinary procedures; Investors in People; 'buddies' and mentoring; job security; impact on motivation

Incentives: remuneration; performance-related pay; incentive schemes, eg commission, bonuses; discounts; holiday entitlement; pension schemes; perks, eg company cars, free meals, uniform provided; opportunities for promotion and progression; impact on motivation

Training: induction; training opportunities; appraisals; impact on motivation

Grading criteria

P1 describe career opportunities for four sectors of the travel and tourism industry and produce a description of two chosen jobs

You must firstly find out all about the two jobs in terms of the job title, the job role, the main duties and responsibilities, the entry requirements, progression opportunities and other factors such as seasonality, level of pay etc.

P2 produce a personal skills audit in preparation for employment

The personal skills audit should be detailed and include an accurate review of your personal skills, attributes, experience, achievements and qualifications, together with supporting evidence to show how they have been acquired or utilised. You can present the audit as a detailed table or a written review.

P5 describe the factors that contribute to an effective workplace in travel and tourism organisations

The description can be in the form of an article, report or presentation and should include a description of the factors, including the working environment, working relationships, incentives and training as detailed in the Content section. Whichever method is selected, it should include relevant industry examples.

M1 compare two jobs in the travel and tourism industry taking into account the entry levels and opportunities for promotion and progression

You must make a comparison against all the aspects identified for P1. For example, the entry requirements for an overseas representative usually include a basic level of a foreign language whereas there is no such requirement for a travel agent. There will be huge differences between the working hours for these two jobs but similarities in that both have to deal with customers.

M3 explain how different travel and tourism organisations motivate staff in the workplace

'To explain' means to make clear, and easy to understand, how the different travel and tourism organisations motivate their staff. This explanation follows on from P5 where you have described the factors that contribute to an effective workplace. Relevant industry examples should be included to support your explanation.

D1 evaluate your own suitability for a chosen job and prepare an action plan to meet all training and development needs

To evaluate your own suitability for a chosen job means that you must identify, from the job description and person specification, the vocational skills, personal skills, qualifications and experience required for the job. You will need to have produced a personal skills audit (P2) and matched this to the criteria for the job and assessed your suitability for the chosen job. You will then be required to prepare an action plan to meet your identified training and development needs in order to meet the requirements for the job.

D2 analyse the factors that contribute to an effective workplace, highlighting good practice from different travel and tourism organisations

'To analyse' means to study something closely and carefully and to make conclusions from this study. For example, a factor that contributes to an effective workplace could be that an organisation uses 'flexi time' hours of work and that this is useful for working parents and for those who want to avoid travelling to work in peak times. You would then need to provide an example from the travel and tourism industry, ie a named organisation that has introduced 'flexi time'.

JOB OPPORTUNITIES IN THE TRAVEL AND TOURISM INDUSTRY

This section focuses on Learning outcomes 1 and 3 and prepares you for Grading criteria P1, P2, M1 and D1. The unit provides you with the opportunity to investigate the range of jobs available on completion of the BTEC National in Travel and Tourism. Some jobs will be available to you immediately after the course and others after a further period of study at a higher level or after a period of related employment.

We have provided you with activities, articles and discussion topics to enable you to investigate career opportunities, select two jobs that interest you and compare the two jobs, taking into account the entry levels and opportunities for promotion and progression. We have also provided you with guidance for identifying and developing your skills in preparation for employment in your chosen career. We have included a template for you to produce a personal skills audit and action plan to meet your training and development needs.

ACTIVITY 1

Task 1

With a partner, select four sectors that interest you from the list below:

- Travel agents (business and leisure)
- Airlines
- Airports
- Accommodation
- Ferries and cruise ships
- Tourist attractions
- Tour operations
- Rail and coach.

Using the Internet, trade magazines and local newspapers, investigate what jobs are available. You may wish to draw up a table with headings such as 'Job title', 'Qualifications required' and 'Salary'.

www.traveljobsearch.com
www.travelindustryjobs.co.uk
www.jobsintravelandtourism.co.uk
www.voovs.com

The following textbooks will also be useful:

Working Tourism: The UK, Europe and Beyond – for Seasonal and Permanent Staff by Verite Reily Collins, published by Kogan Page (2004)

Careers and Jobs in Travel and Tourism by Verite Reily Collins, published by Kogan Page (2004)

Task 2

As a class, discuss your findings, particularly the number of jobs that are available in certain sectors. For example, you will probably have found a huge number of available positions in retail and business travel. Why do you think this sector has so many vacancies? After your discussions, you should individually describe the career opportunities within your four selected sectors, perhaps in the format of a leaflet for each of the sectors. Or, alternatively, you could make a poster or a display for each of the sectors.

ACTIVITY 2

Task 1

You should now select two jobs that you are likely to apply for after completion of the BTEC National and produce a description of these jobs. These should be much more detailed and comprehensive descriptions than the descriptions in Activity 1. You may find that others in the group select the same jobs as you, in which case you should share your findings, but make sure that your descriptions are individual.

To help you to select the two jobs, you can read the extract from the First Choice website below.

First Choice is a fully integrated travel and tourism organisation owning and operating the following areas of business:

- Tour operations (Head Office and overseas)
- Retail travel
- Business travel
- Contact centres
- Airline (flight and reservations).

First Choice recently merged with Thomson TUI. This merger has resulted in these two organisations being one of the largest single integrated travel companies in the world.

Passionate about travel

As a leading leisure travel company we're passionate about giving our customers an experience which leaves them wanting to travel with First Choice time and time again. To achieve this, our people put the customer first in everything that they do, constantly aiming to exceed their expectations. This service ethos extends further than just to those of us that directly deal with external customers, it also applies internally. If this sounds like something that you want to be part of – you may want to consider a career with us!

Our customers' journey with us starts the minute they pick up one of our brochures, perhaps in one of our welcoming First Choice Travel Shops or Holiday Hypermarkets. Our travel consultants, whether it be face-to-face or over the phone, always go the extra mile to find the perfect holiday. Alternatively, some of our customers may choose to buy their holiday or through our user-friendly website. The channels are many.

Then there's the important experience in the air. Our customers are safely flown to the destination of their choice by one of First Choice Airways' experienced pilots, whilst everything in-flight is made special through our unique Star Class service concept, provided by our glamorous and helpful cabin crew.

After touchdown there's nothing better than being welcomed by one of our friendly resort representatives – always happy to help. They know how much our customers have looked forward to a well-earned break and will do everything they can to make it as special as possible.

To ensure that we offer our customers what they want, we carefully research their needs and desires to be able to offer matching destinations, properties, products and services. We continually improve our offering to ensure that it's the very best. At First Choice we think of ourselves as innovative and we do things a little bit different (and better!). As a result many of our products and services are exclusive to us – something which we're very proud of.

Of course, to make people's holiday dreams come true there's also lots happening behind the scenes at First Choice. We regularly have a range of exciting opportunities in functions like Finance, Human Resources, Marketing, E-Commerce and Engineering Services, to mention but a few areas.

If you're passionate about travel and interested in giving customers the best service possible, whether internally or externally, please have a look at our current First Choice Vacancies.

http://www.firstchoice4jobs.co.uk/fe/tpl_firstchoice01.asp?newms=info7

Task 2

Divide into small groups and discuss the advantages of working for a fully integrated travel organisation such as First Choice, particularly in relation to opportunities for progression and promotion. Give a short presentation to the rest of the class with what you find.

ACTIVITY 3

Task 1

Read the following two job descriptions and look particularly at the entry requirements for each role and make comparisons between the two jobs.

RECEPTIONIST IN A SKI RESORT

You never forget the memories you make whilst you're working with Crystal. The rush as you speed down an Alpine slope. The friendships you forge with your work mates. The exhilaration as you walk out into the crisp, clear mountain air each morning. At Crystal, the leading ski and boarding holiday specialists, you won't just help customers have amazing experiences – you'll have them, too.

Of course, you'll give 100% to your guests every minute you're working: helpful, friendly and welcoming. You might be letting a mum know about our crèche facilities or giving a group of students the lowdown on the local nightlife. Whoever comes to reception, the help you give will make sure that they enjoy their holiday even more. Never afraid of hard work, you'll also be ready to pitch in and help with clearing the tables at dinner time and keeping the hotel spic and span.

You have the most important qualification of all for this role – a warm, outgoing personality. You know how to chat to anyone (the ability to speak the local language would be a big plus) and your helpful attitude shines through. You'll need to have five GCSEs and also have good IT and admin skills, plus, ideally, some customer-service and waiting experience. You'll help to create a welcoming environment that our guests will want to return to again and again. In return for all your talents, you'll get the chance to work – and play – in the heart of the mountains.

Crystal Holidays

The public face of an airline – opportunities at Gatwick

The check-in staff are some of the most important people at an airport.

We are a growing and successful company who supply check-in staff to the world's top airlines, at international airports throughout the UK. We can offer you a great future with excellent benefits including subsidised air travel. But, first, see whether you think you would be suited for the job. Do you see yourself:

- welcoming people to their check-in
- dealing with passengers and luggage
- issuing boarding cards
- answering queries in stressful situations
- escorting passengers to the aircraft
- working in a friendly, close-knit team?

If you have answered 'Yes' to the above, then you may be who we are looking for. See if you fit our major criteria. Do you:

- live close to Gatwick Airport (within one hour)
- own a car and have a clean license
- want to undertake shift work including weekends
- hold a valid UK passport with at least six months validity
- feel confident about having a full security check
- have good health (colour blindness is prohibitive)?

We hope you are still answering 'Yes'. If so, we would be pleased to hear from you. Salaries start at £7.80 per hour, rising with experience and unsociable hours, and we offer subsidised meals and some travel allowances. Full training in health and safety, security issues and aviation rules and regulations will be provided.

In small groups, discuss and compare the opportunities for promotion and progression that these two jobs are likely to offer. You should include in-house training opportunities and development through further and higher education. You will need to undertake some further research for this aspect and will probably need to ask your tutor for guidance.

Task 2

Look back at Activity 1 and the list of job opportunities that you discovered. Now select two jobs that most interest you and where you think you could achieve employment, either immediately after your BTEC National or after a further course of study or a period of employment.

For example, if you wish to apply for Air Cabin Crew at 18 years of age it is unlikely you would be accepted. A course of study specific to air cabin crew would be advantageous immediately after your BTEC National, or a period of employment in which you are developing aviation-related customer service skills, perhaps working as an airline passenger service agent at your local airport, or both. Your application for Air Cabin Crew employment would be more likely to be successful if these two options were highlighted on your CV.

Task 3

Once you have selected your two chosen jobs, work with others who have made the same selections in order to fully investigate these positions. You should make a template with the following headings and gather evidence from websites and company literature to enable you to compare the jobs:

- Job title
- Role
- Main duties and responsibilities
- Entry requirements
- Potential for progression
- Other factors, eg seasonality, temporary or fixed-term contract, working hours, level of pay, job perks.

You should focus the detail of your comparisons on entry requirements and opportunities for promotion and progression. To do this you should ensure that you have sufficient detail as follows:

Entry requirements:

- Qualifications
- Personal skills and attributes
- Experience
- Other factors, eg age, location, CRB disclosures for working with children.

Progression:

- Opportunities for promotion and progress
- Training
- Further and higher education.

ACTIVITY 4

Personal Skills Audit and Development Plan

Task 1

You have investigated career opportunities in the travel and tourism industry and researched two jobs that interest you. You now need to select one job from the two: one that you are more likely to pursue at the end of your course. Identify the skills required for that job and list them under these four skill areas:

- Vocational skills
- Personal skills (attributes)
- Qualifications and achievements (include other factors, eg CRB)
- Experience.

Copy out the template below to help you. If possible, word-process the template, then you can expand it as you need to. Now, on your own, complete the first section, ie 'Skills required for the job'.

SKILLS AUDIT AND DEVELOPMENT PLAN – Vocational Skills	
Job title:	
1 Vocational skills required for the job	
2 Own vocational skills	
3 Vocational skills you need to develop	
4 How and by when will you do this?	

Task 2

With a colleague, review your own level of skill, your qualifications, achievements and experience and complete the second section of the template, ie 'Own skills'.

SKILLS AUDIT AND DEVELOPMENT PLAN – Personal Skills (Attributes)	
Job title:	
1 Personal skills required for the job	
2 Own personal skills	
3 Personal skills you need to develop	
4 How and by when will you do this?	

If you need help to identify your own skills, complete the following tasks 3, 4 and 5.

Task 3

Thinking about your vocational skills

Read and discuss the following with a colleague:

Skills are something that you acquire and develop with time. You are using and developing life skills all the time, not just in the workplace. Don't underestimate the many skills you have acquired over the years.

For example, have you ever had to:

- work to a deadline?
- take responsibility?
- make decisions?
- work with other people?
- deal with new situations?
- solve problems?
- budget your finances?
- communicate with other people?

All of these activities involve skills. The term **transferable skills** is often used.

> **Transferable skills** are skills that you have acquired that can be transferred from one career or situation to another – for example, decision making, planning, teamwork, using information technology (IT). Employers will be keen to know what transferable skills you can bring to the job.

Here are some examples of skills that you might have:

communication	numeracy	using IT
public speaking	first aid	interpersonal
caring for others	languages	selling
motivating others	creativity	organisational
negotiating	managing tasks	teamwork
working with others	problem solving	delegating
managing your time	decision making	taking responsibility.

Communication, working with others and problem solving are very important skill areas for most jobs in travel, and employers will attach particular importance to these.

The wider the range of skills you possess, the better prepared you will be to meet the varied demands of working in the travel industry. The following activity will help you to identify the skills that you have used in the past.

Using the lists above as examples, start to identify your hobbies, interests, achievements and work experiences and the skills you have used:

Hobbies and Interests:	Skills used:

Achievements (not just academic, eg raising money for charity, sporting achievements, Duke of Edinburgh Award etc):	Skills used:

Work experiences:	Skills used:

Task 4

Thinking about your personal skills

The travel industry is a 'people industry' and you need to possess personal qualities or attributes that will help you in your day-to-day dealings with others. There are many qualities that an employer could be looking for in a new member of staff. They will be looking for staff with a good balance of personal qualities that can be applied effectively to deal with a wide range of duties.

If an employer in the travel and tourism industry were to make up a wish list of personal qualities, the list would include many of the following:

confident	friendly	trustworthy
supportive	motivated	lively
fair	creative	sociable
honest	calm	sensible
outgoing	optimistic	enthusiastic
tactful	approachable	responsible
committed	assertive	ambitious
efficient	caring	considerate
determined	hard-working	organised
conscientious	reliable	bubbly
flexible	fun	

Ask a colleague to circle those that they think you possess. They can add to the list if they wish!

Discuss with your colleague and identify where you think you could develop and change to become a very employable person in the travel industry.

Task 5

Thinking about customer service skills

Discuss the following with a colleague:

Many of the skills you may have identified above are people-based skills, collectively known as customer service skills. Most jobs in the travel and tourism industry require you to have excellent customer service skills.

Customer service skills include:

- Listening
- Communicating information
- Advising
- Resolving conflicts
- Handling complaints
- Organising
- Caring
- Managing tasks and responsibilities
- Meeting customer needs.

Are you familiar with the word **empathy**?

To have empathy with your customers you will be able to put yourself in their shoes and see things from their point of view. It is much easier to deliver a high standard of customer service if you can empathise with your customers.

Customer service skills are very important when you are working in a customer-focused industry like the travel industry. In these days of fierce competition, offering an excellent standard of customer service can be the one thing that sets one company apart from the others. It is vital that you fully appreciate the importance of customer service in all areas of the travel industry and have sufficient work or work-related experience so that you can demonstrate your knowledge of, and skill in, customer service during an interview. Employers will be trying to find out if you have the drive and commitment to be the best.

Think of an occasion when you have received an excellent standard of customer service.

Tell your colleague about your example. Explain what it was that made this service so memorable.

Most of us will only remember excellent customer service when someone has done something that has exceeded our expectations. Are you willing to put yourself out to exceed the customers' expectations? If so, then you could be just what employers are looking for, but you will need to prove to a prospective employer that you possess these skills and it is very hard to develop customer service skills without experience of working with the public.

Discuss how you will further develop your customer service skills and how you will prove to a prospective employer that you have the required skills.

Try to evaluate your suitability for a selected job by recognising your own strengths and weaknesses in relation to the detailed roles and responsibilities of the job. Below is a case study featuring a job description including entry requirements for a Holiday Representative.

With a colleague, read the case study below, then copy and complete the table (already started for you on page 88). In the right-hand column, you should end up with more 'Yes' entries to establish that you are suitable for the job.

Once you have completed this exercise you should turn your attention to your selected job and formulate your action plan by matching your skills against those required for the job and identify any gaps. You will need to research any further training and educational needs that you feel would be beneficial, such as vocational courses specific to the job or higher education. You should complete the **third and fourth sections** of the template, ie skills you need to develop/achieve and how and when you will do this.

Tasks 3, 4 and 5 will have also helped you to identify the skills you need to develop.

CASE STUDY

HOLIDAY REPRESENTATIVE – **Job description**

A holiday representative is responsible for looking after groups of clients on package holidays at resorts.

Their main priority is to ensure that clients enjoy their holiday and that everything runs as smoothly as possible for them. As the public face of the tour operator, they must create an excellent first impression and continue to provide an outstanding service to clients throughout the duration of their stay.

The role involves holding 'welcome' meetings, handling complaints and resolving problems as they arise.

Holiday representatives are often also responsible for selling resort excursions and additional services, such as car hire.

Typical work activities

Work activities may vary slightly depending on the tour operator, but will typically include:

- meeting guests at the airport;
- escorting guests to their accommodation;
- organising and hosting welcome meetings (often for up to 200 people);
- selling and organising resort excursions and other activities;
- selling car hire and other services;
- responding to clients' queries (this may involve being on duty for set times each day);
- handling client issues, such as: lost luggage or passports; allegations of theft or other crimes; problems with rooms; health problems, injuries, or even deaths;
- dealing with unforeseen 'non-client' problems, eg flight delays, coach strikes;
- resolving any conflict with or between clients;
- establishing and maintaining relationships with local hoteliers, apartment owners, agents and travel companies;
- maintaining an in-depth knowledge of the resort and the local area in order to answer clients' questions;
- keeping up to date with local events and activities, which may be of interest to clients;
- maintaining an in-depth knowledge of all the excursions offered;
- accompanying customers on excursions and acting as a guide;
- taking part in and organising daytime and evening entertainment;
- checking hotel standards and safety procedures;
- keeping basic accounts and records, and writing reports.

HOLIDAY REPRESENTATIVE – **Entry requirements**

Working as a holiday representative does not usually require a degree or any specific qualifications. Relevant skills and personal qualities are more important. Most tour operators seek candidates with experience of working in a customer service role.

A minimum age is often stipulated. This is usually 21 for overseas representatives and 19 for children's representatives, although it can be 18 for some tour operators.

Pre-entry experience of selling, dealing with large groups and working/travelling overseas is desirable, but not usually essential.

Potential candidates will need to show evidence of the following:

- communication skills (both oral and written);
- an outgoing, confident and energetic personality;
- stamina and enthusiasm;
- listening and negotiation skills;
- a commitment to high levels of customer service;
- team working ability;
- a good sense of humour;
- planning and organisational skills;

- flexibility;
- common sense;
- a friendly and approachable manner;
- problem-solving ability;
- a hands-on and proactive approach.

The ability to speak a second language (preferably European) is a further bonus.

Most tour operators require completion of an online application form. These can be found on their respective career websites.

From 1 October 2006 it will be illegal to discriminate against candidates on age grounds but, in practice, age may continue to be used in selection criteria by some employers. Most of the larger tour operators offer a wide variety of packages, some of which may be more suited to mature applicants. For more information on equality and diversity in the job market and how to handle discrimination, see the AGCAS publication *Handling Discrimination*.

Extract from the 'Prospects' website: the UK's official graduate careers website (www.prospects.ac.uk).

Job Activity	Skills Required	How used	Could I do this?
Meeting guests at the airport	Communication Outgoing, confident and energetic personality A friendly and approachable manner	Call out names, check on list (spellings and pronunciations) Need to be confident to stand in the airport and sort out the guests Need to portray a friendly image	
Organising and hosting 'welcome' meetings			
Dealing with unforeseen problems, eg flight delays, coach strikes			
Resolving any conflict with, or between, clients			
Keeping basic accounts, records and writing reports			

88

SKILLS AUDIT AND DEVELOPMENT PLAN – Qualifications and Achievements (and other factors)	
Job title:	
1 Qualifications and achievements required for the job (include other required factors)	
2 Own qualifications and achievements (include other required factors)	
3 Qualifications and further achievements required (include other required factors)	
4 How and by when will you do this?	

SKILLS AUDIT AND DEVELOPMENT PLAN – Experience	
Job title:	
1 Experience required for the job	
2 Own experience	
3 Experience you need to achieve	
4 How and by when will you do this?	

THE TRAVEL AND TOURISM WORKING ENVIRONMENT

This section focuses on Learning outcome 4 and prepares you for Grading criteria P5, M3 and D2. The unit provides you with the opportunity to examine the factors that contribute to an effective workplace in the Travel and Tourism industry.

The jobs available to you are wide ranging in terms of working environment. You may be working in an airport at check-in and your shift may start at 0400 hrs, or as a dispatcher working airside on the ramp in dangerous conditions and in all weathers. You may be working for an airline on short-haul or long-haul flights, working long days but sometimes staying over in luxury hotels in exotic places.

You may be working as a holiday representative or a children's representative and based on a campsite, living in a tent or a mobile home, or living in an apartment in a seaside resort, or you may be away from home for over six months at a time, working long hours, often on your own.

You may be based on a cruise ship for eight months, living in a small cabin but experiencing wonderful ports of call, or travelling back and forth between the south of England and France on a ferry, or travelling north and south on a train.

You may, however, be based in an office environment, working for a tour operator or in a shop environment, working as a travel agent. If you enter this industry you have to be prepared for extraordinary, exciting and challenging working environments in the UK, overseas, on the seas or in the air.

In the activities that follow, you will investigate the factors that contribute to an effective workplace in travel and tourism organisations. You will work towards an explanation of how organisations motivate their staff and an analysis of the factors that contribute to an effective working environment and provide examples of good practice.

ACTIVITY 5

There are many factors that contribute to an effective workplace. In small groups, select a job from the list below (each group should select a different job):

- Air cabin crew
- Travel agent
- Passenger service agent (airport)
- Holiday representative overseas
- Receptionist at a visitor attraction.

Task 1

The working environment impacts on employee motivation. In your groups, discuss the typical working environment for your selected job and how this can affect employee motivation. The chart below for a Ski Chalet Assistant is an example. Make your own chart on a flip chart or poster and complete it for the job role that you have chosen. Display your poster and discuss it with the whole group.

Job: Ski Chalet Assistant

Working Environment	Negative impact on motivation	Positive impact on motivation
Location	A long way from home Cold and snowy	Ski resort Snow Holiday environment
Working Conditions	Sharing a room with someone you don't know Living in a chalet with strangers No privacy	Living in a nice chalet Living with lots of people Getting to know new people
Hours of work	Long hours	Time off to ski
Health and safety	Danger of avalanches Open fires Ski accidents	Personal insurance provided
Equipment	Using unfamiliar equipment in the chalet	Provided with ski clothing, working clothing and cheap ski rental
Resources	Limited cooking resources	Provided with everything we need
Social Events	Too tired to join in	Company provides one night off to socialise Can socialise with the customers
Other	Long season	A whole winter away from home with opportunities to ski for free

Task 2

Working relationships can impact on employee motivation both negatively and positively. Select at least two different factors per group from the list below and discuss them in relation to employee motivation. For example, discuss how different management styles may affect employees. Some employees like to be told exactly what to do, while others welcome the opportunity to work on their own initiative and an autocratic manager could inhibit their creativity and flair. Think of examples from your own work experience or ask family and friends about their experiences in relation to motivation at work.

- Management style
- Teamwork
- Job roles and lines of responsibility
- Channels of communication
- Equal opportunities
- Pay
- Legislative requirements
- Grievance and disciplinary procedures
- Investors in people
- Buddies and mentoring
- Job security.

Make a note of your discussions and decide on two examples, one for each of your factors listed above, and present these examples to the full group.

Task 3

Have you heard about the theories of Maslow and Hertberz? These are related to motivation in work. You can find explanations in textbooks and websites. The following are suggestions:

http://hosting.menanet.net/~khair1/khair1/Theory%20of%20Motivation.htm
http://www.bbc.co.uk/dna/h2g2/A2860346
http://www.training-manager.co.uk/documents/mtdmotivation.pdf
http://www.markville.ss.yrdsb.edu.on.ca/teacher/business/business/12/BOH4M/Units/unit_5/motivational_theories.ppt#256,1,Motivational Theories

Divide into four groups and find out more about each of the following theorists (selecting one theorist per group):

- Maslow
- Hertberz
- Douglas McGregor – Managerial Style Theory X/Theory Y
- B F Skinner – behaviour modification

Create a short handout that introduces and explains the work of each of the theorists. Understanding the theory behind employee motivation is an important part of moving towards achieving M3 when it comes to your assignment.

Task 4

A very important factor that can contribute to an effective workplace is classed under the heading of 'incentives'. We all need some incentive to do better and most organisations have a range of incentives to encourage things like:

- Increased production
- Increased retention (related to length of service)
- Improved performance
- Improved service levels
- Improved satisfaction levels of staff

- Improved satisfaction levels of customers
- Ensuring that motivation levels are high.

Working in pairs or threes, use a word processor to design a table like the one opposite so that you can expand the boxes to give very full and detailed answers. The first section has been completed as an example.

Incentive	How does this motivate an employee?	If this incentive is not present, is not above average or is badly organised, how might this impact on motivation?
Remuneration – a good level of pay in keeping with the job	Pay is usually the most motivating factor because it is why we all go to work, and the better pay we earn, the better lifestyle we have.	If pay is less than in other organisations we might want to move, and if we are always on the look out for a new job we won't be very satisfied and therefore very motivated. However, if all the other factors are good, we might stay because the other factors are also important and motivate us more than the pay, eg the holiday discounts, the location, nice colleagues, praise and appreciation from the manager.
Pay scales where employee pay rises each year to the next band		
Performance-related pay		
Commission on sales		
Bonuses at the end of the year dependent on sales or performance		
Discounts on products sold within the organisation, eg holidays		
A good level of holiday entitlement with an increase for each year of service		
A good pension scheme where the employer contribution is high		
Perks, such as a company car, free meals, a uniform		
Good opportunities for promotion and progression		
Good level of ongoing training provided		
Effective appraisal system in place		

As a general group discussion, using the white-board, compare your responses with the different theorists. Are your responses in line with one or more of the theorists or not?

ACTIVITY 6

Having examined and discussed the factors that contribute to an effective workplace in Activity 5 and explored various motivation theories, you should now seek real examples of how different travel and tourism organisations motivate staff in the workplace.

Task 1

Read the following job description and list the incentives, in order of preference, that would appeal to you and have a positive impact on your motivation to work for the company. If you visit the First Choice website (www.firstchoice4jobs.co.uk) you will find that they list many incentives and motivational factors for all their jobs. Discuss:

- Why do they offer so many incentives?
- Why is it good for the company to offer these incentives?
- Are there advantages in being a large fully integrated company in relation to offering incentives and motivational factors?

Job details (taken from www.firstchoice4jobs.co.uk)
Assistant Manager – Southampton

Region: North West

Business Area: Retail

At a Glance:
Drawing on your supervisory experience, you'll assist the manager in the day-to-day running of the shop ensuring that the profitability is maximised and the company's high standards are achieved.
Requests for flexible working hours may be considered for this position.

What You'll Be Doing:

For our customer

As part of the management team, you'll create and encourage a positive impression of First Choice Retail through leading by example in every area of customer service. You will be genuine and enthusiastic and show the customer that you value them by actively seeking to enhance information given to them by yourself and your team at every opportunity.

For our company

Assisting with the overall running of this travel shop, and assuming responsibility of the sales and/or foreign exchange departments when required, your strong supervisory and management skills will enable you to lead by example and develop your team to meet targets. You'll ensure that all areas are resourced appropriately with members of the team that can provide expert travel advice and services to all customers.

What We're Looking For:
Essential

- Target sales experience

Desirable

- Experience of managing staff at a supervisory level
- Retail travel knowledge
- Knowledge of retail travel IT systems

What We Can Offer You:
- Competitive salary with excellent bonus/commission earning potential
- Excellent career prospects
- Initial and ongoing training

- Yearly incremental holiday concessions
- Generous discounts off First Choice products
  (including for Friends & Family discount)
- Heavily discounted travel from various travel companies
- First Choice contributory pension scheme after 12 months
- Generous holiday entitlement
- Life Assurance
- Education (after 1 yrs service)
- Uniform

Task 2

Read the following (fictional) Top Tier Travel job description and then make notes and discuss:

- What type of person would this job appeal to?
- Do you think there would be some negative factors within this type of working environment?
- What would motivate you the most in this job?

TOP TIER TRAVEL NEED SALES CONSULTANTS – LONDON

What's the job?

You will be working with major commercial and individual clients and providing them with a complete travel package – advising, guiding and booking a range of services to suit their diverse needs. It might be a world cruise for a family taken over a two-month period; it might be a quick trip to the opera in New York; it might be bringing together fifty people from around the globe to attend a conference; it might be anything!

What's special?

As a member of a busy team, you won't be just a small part of the process. It is more like running your own agency, with your own client-base, targets, opportunities and potential. Each individual within TTT is given the rewards to match their achievement. Your success… it's up to you.

What about Top Tier Travel?

Top Tier Travel (TTT) is one of the world's leading travel agencies. We operate on the high street under a brand name, but much of our work is at the corporate level. We have won numerous awards, not only for our agency work but also for the care and attention we give to our staff. We have offices in eleven cities in the UK and affiliated companies throughout the world.

What's the deal?

- Full time employment
- Five week's holiday
- Based in London (West End)
- Salary minimum £22,000
- Commission potential unlimited
- Health insurance
- Gym membership
- Huge travel discounts

What do we want?

We want your energy, your passion for travel (that you can communicate to your clients) and we want you to learn quickly. Good with people, excellent at communicating, willing to work hard and comfortable with tough targets… these things go without saying.

What to do next?

Decide for yourself that you have got the ambition, energy and enterprise for this tough and demanding role – then convince us. We want to hear from you.

Task 3

Read the following case studies and answer the questions. You can work in small groups or pairs.

CASE STUDY A

Maddy has been working for one year as a Travel Consultant for a multiple travel agency that is part of a large integrated company. The incentives offered are very good and include:

- Competitive salary with excellent bonus/commission on sales
- Excellent career prospects into management
- Initial and ongoing training
- Yearly incremental holiday concessions
- Generous discounts for own products (including Friends and Family discount)
- Heavily discounted travel from various travel companies
- Contributory pension scheme after 12 months
- Generous holiday entitlement
- Life Assurance
- Education (after 1 yrs service)
- Uniform.

There are four other Travel Consultants, an Assistant Manager and a Manager plus an Administration Assistant. The shop opens six days per week and each member of the team has one day off during the week with every other Saturday. Maddy enjoys her job but does not like one of the other Consultants, Sue, who has been working for the organisation for four years; Maddy is on the same rota as Sue and is mentored by Sue. Sue is very friendly with the Assistant Manager. Maddy is the youngest and least experienced and so finds it difficult to be assertive with Sue. Sue, on the other hand, is very bossy and always gives Maddy the least satisfying jobs and nearly always manages to interfere when Maddy is about to close a sale so that Sue ends up booking the customer and taking the commission. Maddy has tried to talk to the Manager about this but the Manager always refers this back to the Assistant Manager who says that Sue is only trying to help and that Maddy is not very good at closing sales.

Maddy realises that she has a future with the company but wants to leave as she is unhappy and not very motivated. In fact, she now does not look forward to going to work.

Questions for Case Study A:

Explain why, even with all the incentives listed, Maddy is not motivated to stay with the company, and how the company could ensure that Maddy remains motivated. Who is at fault? Is it the systems in place or the management or both? Do you think this happens in other organisations?

CASE STUDY B

Paul has been employed for ten weeks as a Holiday Representative with a large tour operator and is based in Ibiza. He has been allocated six hotels in San Antonia Bay. He is sharing accommodation with two other reps, Jessica and Martin. They all have their own bedrooms and share the bathroom, living room and kitchen. They are all in their first season. Paul is enjoying the job and finds it very challenging and has found the long hours very tiring and he is not coping very well with having to do his own washing and cooking.

All this is not helped by Jessica and Martin being very noisy, drinking and partying most nights and inviting people back to the apartment. Paul's health is suffering and he constantly feels unwell and very tired. He has been late on a number of occasions for his 'welcome' meetings and seems to have lost his enthusiasm. He is a good salesman and, initially, his sales figures for excursions and car hire were very good but now he can't be bothered.

All new reps with this company are allocated an experienced rep to mentor them and they are supposed to meet up at least once per week to discuss progress and any concerns. All new reps are also scheduled to meet with their Supervisor once every two weeks and after the first six weeks to have an appraisal, followed by one after 12 weeks. The system in place also schedules a once-a-month meeting for all new reps with the Resort Manager.

Because of staff shortages and other problems, the procedures have not been followed. Paul has only seen his mentor once a week for the first three weeks, he has only seen his Supervisor once (two weeks after starting) and he has not had his appraisal.

Paul is really down, does not know who to speak to and so has decided to pack his bags and ask for a flight home.

Questions for Case Study B:

What are the factors that have de-motivated Paul?

What is the point of having a supportive system in place if it is not used?

Who is at fault?

What are the negative impacts on the company if Paul leaves?

CASE STUDY C

Tom has been employed by a small coach tour operator in their Head Office as a Trainee Product Manager for five months. He is enjoying his job and, whilst the company is quite small, employing 20 staff, it is a family-run operation. The office is well furnished, with adequate heating and air conditioning. There are three floors, with reservations and customer service on the ground floor, marketing, product design and operations on the second floor, and the managing director, the finance director and the operators and IT manager are on the top floor.

Tom is paid a trainee salary, which rises every six months, and in two years he will be on a good salary with the possibility of a bonus, subject to sales targets being met across the company. The company has released him to do his Certificate in Marketing at the local college. He is working closely with three Product Managers, one for the UK, one for the European Tours and one who is responsible for new developments.

He has been given a new area of development, a tour by rail to Switzerland, and he has been researching all the aspects and reporting back to the Product Development Manager. He has been given support and also praise for progress so far. He is due to have his first appraisal next week and he has been given a document to complete before the appraisal takes place, which helps him to identify his strengths, his weaknesses, what he has enjoyed the best, what he has enjoyed the least, any training needs he has and where he wants to go within the company.

Tom has also been given the opportunity to join one of the UK tours and one of the European tours to help to familiarise himself with operating procedures and issues.

The Managing Director called him to his office last week to have a chat over a cup of coffee and encouraged Tom to talk about the company, his job and progress so far.

Next month all the staff have been invited on a weekend tour to one of the UK hotels used within their tour operation. This gives the staff the opportunity of familiarising themselves with the hotel and also to mix in a relaxed social environment.

Tom is very happy in his job even though he knows he could have started on a much higher salary with other tour operators.

Questions for Case Study C:

Why is Tom happy in the job?

What are the main factors that are keeping Tom motivated?

Task 4

There are many examples of motivation techniques used within travel and tourism organisations and you should now have the knowledge to be able to analyse the factors that contribute to an effective workplace. You should now try and find examples of good practice by reading the *Travel Trade Gazette*, the *Travel Weekly* and ask those working in travel about what motivates them most to stay with their organisation.

Case Study C provided a good example in relation to the free weekend trip for the staff. Working in small groups, you should find a similar example and showcase this to the rest of the group, analysing why your example motivates the staff and contributes to an effective workplace.

You should now appreciate the incentives and motivational factors that companies offer their employees to keep them satisfied and loyal and so maintain a happy workforce. When seeking work in the travel and tourism industry, you should now be able to analyse the factors that contribute to an effective workplace and this should help you to make those important decisions of who you want to work for and the incentives and motivational factors you would want from your employer.

This unit focuses on grading criteria P1, M1 and D1.

Unit overview

The retail and business travel sector has a key part to play within the travel and tourism industry. Constantly evolving to meet the ever-changing needs of its customers, it is an exciting industry with a world full of destinations on offer to the consumer. This unit explores the operation of both retail and business travel agents. It highlights the relationship between these agents and other sectors of the travel and tourism industry. The unit also looks at the different types of retail and business agents that exist and the trade associations, licensing, memberships and legal frameworks within which they work.

Advances in technology have had a major impact on the operation of retail and business agents. This has affected the operation of the agency, the ways in which customers now make bookings, commission levels, distribution, and methods of communication used by agents. The unit investigates the different advances in technology and their impacts, including dynamic packaging and home-working.

The retail sector is particularly competitive and these agents fight to have the competitive edge in a market that is already saturated. You will look at the strategies adopted to enable agents to retain and grow their market shares; these include offering low-deposit bookings or free child places.

For both retail and business travel, exploring and meeting customer needs is a crucial part of the service they offer. This unit involves you in selecting different products and services to meet customers' needs. In addition, you will understand the process of making secondary sales or 'up-selling' to clients in order to increase commission and meet sales targets. This will enable you to gain knowledge of the range of products and services offered by retail and business agents as well as to develop awareness of sales techniques used within the industry.

The unit also develops practical skills in presenting itineraries that meet customers' varied and sometimes complex needs.

In this Study Guide the activities relate to Learning outcome 1. This learning outcome is concerned with understanding how organisations operate in the ever-changing and complex retail and business travel environment. You will need to read the travel press and keep up-to-date with changing practices, trends, new concepts, the latest mergers and take-overs. This is an interesting section, where you will develop knowledge of how to plan and organise your own travel and holiday needs and make best use of the many and varied booking options available.

Learning outcome

1 Understand the retail and business travel environments

Content

1) Understand the retail and business travel environments

Retail agencies: independents; multiples; integrated; e-agents; home workers; role

Business agencies: general business travel; corporate hospitality; incentive travel; e-agent; role

Markets: leisure; business

Products and services: retail, eg holidays; ancillary sales; business, eg scheduled flights, accommodation, ancillary sales

Legal and regulatory framework: trade associations, eg Association of British Travel Agents (ABTA), Association of Train Operating Companies (ATOC); consortia, eg Advantage Travel Centres, Worldchoice; memberships, eg ABTA, International Air Transport Association (IATA); licensing, eg Air Travel Organiser's License (ATOL), rail; legal framework, eg EU Package Travel Regulations, consumer protection, contract law; Financial Services Authority

Relationship: integration (vertical, horizontal); agency agreements; commission levels; preferred operators; racking policies; fiancial bonding

Sectors: accommodation providers; transport providers; ancillary providers, eg insurance, car hire, airport hotels; tour operators

Grading criteria

P1 describe the retail and business travel environment (including the relationship between retail and business travel agents and other sectors of the travel and tourism industry) using examples where appropriate

This means that you should describe all the different parts of the Content for Learning outcome 1. This will set the scene for this unit and provide you with a sound knowledge of the retail and business travel environment and help you to understand the complexities of this environment within the travel industry of today.

M1 explain how relationships operate in the retail and business travel environment and its impact on the travel industry as a whole

'To explain' means to make clear and easy to understand how relationships operate in the retail and business travel environment. 'Environment', in this context, means all the different types of organisations involved, including: retail agencies (independents, multiples, integrated, e-agents, home-workers), business agencies (general business travel, corporate hospitality, incentive travel, e-agent), legal and regulatory framework (trade associations, consortia, memberships, licensing, legislation) and sectors (transport, accommodation, ancillary, tour operations). 'Relationships' include: integration (vertical and horizontal), agency agreements (eg between agency and tour operator), commission levels, preferred operators, racking policies, financial bonding, and booking fees for non-commissionable products.

D1 evaluate the effectiveness of retail and business travel organisations and how they operate in the travel and tourism environment

To meet this criterion, you must firstly have investigated and understood the environment and then explained how organisations operate within it. To 'evaluate' fully you must select a number of organisations and examine how they are operating in today's climate and whether or not they are successful or if they are in decline. For example, you will need to explore trends in bookings and the impact of technology on the traditional retail and business travel agent. How are they responding? Are they able to compete?

THE RETAIL AND BUSINESS TRAVEL ENVIRONMENT

You will have the opportunity to investigate the retail and business travel environment, including the relationship between retail and business travel agents and other sectors of the travel and tourism industry. You will explore the impact of this environment on the industry as a whole and evaluate the effectiveness of retail and business travel agents and their standing in the complex and competitive world of travel.

We have provided you with activities, articles and discussion topics to enable you to explore and examine some of the hot topics emerging in the retail and business travel environment, and pointed the way towards understanding the complexities of this environment. Your research should enable you to evaluate the effectiveness of a range of retail and business travel organisations, explain how they operate and appreciate their status in the industry and in doing so, you will be working towards the higher grades for Outcome 1.

ACTIVITY 1

This activity is designed to help you to explore the retail and business travel environment in an interesting way, by allowing you to investigate actual travel companies.

Task 1

In any town or city throughout the UK you will find a range of different types of travel agencies. The following is a fictitious example:

Howton is a small market town in the north of England. It has two main shopping streets and a population of 25 000. There are six travel agencies in and around the town:

Lunn Poly: a multiple, opened in 1984 as part of the Thomson Holiday Group. Thomson merged with the German company TUI and recently with First Choice to become the biggest travel company in Europe. The shop has a prime high street location and the main focus is leisure travel. As you walk into the shop, the TUI product is racked very prominently.

Horizon Tours and Travel (HTT) is part of a regional retail group and situated within a department store. They have eight other agencies within department stores around the region. They specialise in leisure travel and also operate their own range of UK coach tours. They have a number of beneficial commission arrangements with tour operators. Their overheads are low because of the department store location and they tend to offer some good discounts.

Goodwin's is a regional, privately owned company with ten branches. They offer a mix of travel products including leisure and business travel, airport transfers, and currency. They rack a wide variety of brochures and feature many specialist tour companies. They are well established in the town, with a good reputation and a prime site, opposite Lunn Poly.

Howton Travel is an independent travel agent, a member of the Advantage Travel Consortia. The agency has two very large business accounts for local companies and several smaller business accounts. They specialise in tailor-made and bespoke holidays. They have been established in the town since 1961 and the agency is still owned and managed by the son of the original owner and is situated in a side street just off the main shopping street.

Waterman Travel is an independent agent offering a range of products but specialising in action holidays with a reputation for organising complex itineraries to long-haul destinations such as the Himalayas and Africa. They also have a website and much of their business is via the Internet. The agency is situated on the outskirts of the town with its own car park. The agency opens longer hours than normal: until 7 pm most evenings and on Sunday mornings.

Travelchoice Holiday Hypermarket opened ten years ago on a retail park 3 miles from Howton. This agency is part of First Choice. First Choice has recently merged with TUI. The Holiday Hypermarket is focused on offering a wide range of leisure travel products and services and is open for longer hours than the high street shops.

In small groups, each select a town or city within your region and investigate all the different travel companies in and around your selected town or city and report on these in a similar way to the example provided above, but you should **expand these descriptions to include**:

- What type of agency they are, eg multiple integrated, independent and part of a consortia, independent
- What memberships they have, eg ABTA, IATA
- What licences they hold, eg ATOL, rail
- What products and services they offer and if these are leisure and also business products.

A list is not appropriate: you should include descriptions. For example, you should describe what ABTA is and why some of the agencies are members of this scheme.

You should also include in your description the legal framework for these agencies, eg Package Travel Regulations, consumer protection, contract law and the Financial Services Authority, and you should describe how this legislation impacts on the agencies.

You will probably find a similar mixture of multiples, regional multiples and independents offering a wide variety of products and services including leisure travel, business travel and tours. Produce a handout for the whole class or give a presentation showing what you have found for your chosen town and including the detail as described above.

Task 2

You can already see that there is a huge choice of where and how to book your holiday, and this comes down to personal preference. You may prefer to walk into a local travel agency and spend time with a travel consultant discussing your needs, making decisions and then let them process the booking. You may prefer to contact the local agent by telephone to make your enquiries and process the booking. You may call into the agency later to make your payment or to collect your tickets.

The majority of bookings in the high street agency will be the traditional package holiday selected from a tour operator's brochure such as Thomson, First Choice or one of the smaller companies such as Libra Holidays. Do you know what a package holiday is? The definition is that it includes transport, accommodation and ancillary services, eg transfers to and from the airport to the hotel and the services of a representative.

Using a high street agency is the traditional choice, but is it the cheapest or the best? To help you to understand the choices, firstly find out some prices for the holiday detailed below. Select a package from a large tour operator and a package from a smaller tour operator. Your tutor will help you to understand how to cost a holiday from a brochure. Once you have done this, keep a record of the costs.

> A holiday for two people to Majorca in June, travelling from a local airport, staying in a 4-star hotel in Alcudia with a sea view and with transfers to and from the airport to the hotel.

Task 3

The alternative is to book via the Internet. Over recent years the number of travel companies offering this option has increased. Companies such as lastminute.com and expedia.com are classed as e-agents (sometimes called web-based agents), selling the full range of travel products including flights, accommodation, package holidays and other travel extras such as car-hire and insurance.

Tour operators have, in the past, only sold their package holidays by displaying their brochures in retail travel agents. Many tour operators now offer their own products online, such as Thomson and First Choice. These companies also offer a telephone number into their call centres so that you have a choice of using the online facility for all or part of the booking, or contacting one of their consultants by telephone.

Low-cost scheduled airlines have now entered the marketplace and not only offer their own flights online but also accommodation, car hire, transfers and insurance. They have linked with other online booking companies such as Hotelopia.co.uk for accommodation.

In groups, prepare to book the holiday to Majorca, detailed above, online. Firstly, conduct some research and list up to 20 different travel companies who have a website and where you can book your holiday either over the telephone and/or online. This research will help you to identify the wide range of websites available to the leisure traveller.

Select TWO one-stop websites where you could book the flight, the transfers and the accommodation online. We have provided you with a template and used the easyJet website as an example.

Company	Flight details and cost	Transfer details and cost	Accommodation details and cost
easyJet	Liverpool to Palma depart 05 June at 1315, return 12 June at 1945 Cost: Outbound £49 Inbound £79 + taxes £20 TOTAL COST: £148 pp	Using ATS 4easyJet Airport to Hotel £20 pp Hotel to Airport £20 pp	Using easyJet/Hotelopia President Hotel in Puerto de Alcudia £455 for two people for 7 nights

Other findings:

All the above were undertaken using just the one-stop easyJet website. easyJet have a relationship with ATS (an airline transfer service company) and also with Hotelopia (a hotel booking company). ATS and Hotelopia have their own websites but they have linked with easyJet so that customers can book the transfer and the hotel via the easyJet website.

Also available on the easyJet website in relation to this booking are:
- Airport parking bookings at Liverpool Airport
- Travel insurance
- Car rental in Majorca.

Already, you should be starting to appreciate the relationships between other sectors of the industry and between traditional agents and e-agents. Make notes about these relationships in readiness for working towards M1 and D1. Your research will also have provided you with opportunities to use examples.

Task 4

You should repeat the same exercise for a **business traveller**. From your research you will find that there are web-based companies dedicated to the business customer, dealing with general business, corporate hospitality and incentive travel. These companies serve both the corporate and individual business traveller. In groups, visit the websites of a range of business travel agencies and select one per group to examine more closely. Report back to the rest of the group on their products and services and how they operate with their suppliers and their business customers.

Extracts from two business travel agent websites are shown below:

Welcome to Business Travel Direct at www.btdonline.co.uk

Business Travel Direct makes travel simple, stress-free and cost effective, allowing you to work with suppliers that best suit your corporate needs whether it's through our traditional offline service or our own award-winning website and online travel portal. Backed up with over 35 years experience in the corporate travel market.

Benefits

- Price driven flight searches with over 5 million special fares including 72 low cost carriers
- Earn vouchers toward your holiday when taking advantage of our special Bizzy Fares
- Access to over 180,000 properties from B & B and apartments to luxury 7 star accommodation
- View not just a range of prices but all available car hire companies
- We provide all clients with a personal team to manage their travel needs
- Staff Holiday Club through our own tour operator Letsgo2.com

Total Travel Management Solution

Hogg Robinson Group (HRG) is an international corporate services provider with over 60 years specific corporate (business) travel expertise.

HRG brings a new way of seeing, new ways of working and new ways of delivering superior corporate services to companies across the world.

We listen. We understand. We offer tailored solutions. We deliver impressive results.

At HRG we are dedicated to making sure your company gets maximum value for your corporate travel budget so that you succeed. That's the HRG difference.

Our reputation for service excellence has been proven time and time again. It's not only the many awards we have won over the years that stand testament to this fact, but also our clients. With an impressive portfolio that encompasses multinational corporations and national companies, HRG has long been delivering solutions to some of the most prestigious corporations around the world.

Our business is built on a client-focused approach where our people, technology solutions, processes and procedures revolve around your needs and expectations.

For example, we understand that when making important decisions, you need the complete picture. That's why we can capture data from around the world and deliver timely and relevant information for analysis to your desktop or HRG staff acting on your behalf.

Our expertise is also used to reduce cost in areas from service delivery and strategic supplier negotiations, right through to individual traveller itineraries.

Every year we save our clients millions in travel expenditure and every day we challenge ourselves to improve our performance.

You will probably find that all the business travel agents publish their telephone numbers on their website and so encourage telephone discussions with customers in relation to arrangements for transport, accommodation and other ancillary services. This method provides a more personal service and an opportunity for the customer to fully explain their needs and the agent to recognise these needs and explore the most appropriate options available; business travel itineraries tend to be complex.

The results of your findings will lead you towards understanding the relationships between business travel agents and other sectors of the travel and tourism industry and provide opportunities to use examples.

Task 5

Your research so far will have developed your knowledge of the range of booking options available to customers and the range of products and services offered. Booking options are:

- High-street travel agent
- Direct with the tour operator
- Web-based travel agency
- Low-cost airline.

You need to develop your knowledge to understand and appreciate how these companies operate to offer the travel product.

Flights

You will have noted that the low-cost airlines only offer their own low-cost scheduled flights. The tour operators only offer their own charter flights. The web-based travel agents and the high-street agents offer a range of charter flights and scheduled flights. Some high-street agencies offer to book low-cost scheduled flights for a booking fee.

Do you understand the difference between these types of flights?

- Scheduled
- Low-cost scheduled – economy class only
- Low-cost scheduled – business class only
- Charter.

You will find useful explanations courtesy of:

Word Travels at www.wordtravel.com

The Charter Flight Centre at http://www.charterflights.co.uk/faq.php

You will find useful explanations in all the BTEC National Travel and Tourism textbooks.

Divide into groups and for each type of flight produce a definition and select one airline. Explain the features and benefits of that airline and describe the products and services they offer.

Did you know about low-cost scheduled business-only class airlines? This is a fairly new concept and has emerged because so many business travellers are choosing the flexibility of low-cost scheduled airlines and entrepreneurs have decided to offer these business travellers a dedicated service. If you check out their websites, eg Silverjet, you will be impressed! This is another example of relationships between the different sectors of the industry.

Accommodation

Low-cost scheduled airlines and web-based agencies use hotel booking agencies such as Hotelopia. Tour operators offer hotels already contracted to them as detailed in their brochures. The high-street agent can offer the tour operator product or use a range of hotel booking agencies.

Via the Internet, research the options available to the customer and the travel trade in order to book hotel accommodation.

Using our holiday to Majorca in Task 2, put together your own package by finding the cheapest flight and then the cheapest hotel accommodation and the cheapest transfers. Use separate companies rather than the one-stop-shop.

Compare your prices with the rest of the group. Which group has obtained the cheapest deal?

Are you now starting to realise the complexities of booking a holiday and the relationships between the different sectors of the industry? Make notes to help you to work towards M1 and D1.

Task 6

The legal and regulatory framework in which all agents work helps to protect the consumer. Under the Package Travel, Package Holidays and Package Tours Regulations 1992, the organiser of the package is ultimately responsible for all aspects of the package holiday. There is much debate about whether separate bookings of flights, accommodation and other extras will come under these regulations. In order to understand more about this legal aspect, read the following:

Information from the DTI – The Package Travel Regulations: Question and Answer Guidance for Organisers and Retailers, November 2006.

http://www.dti.gov.uk/files/file35634.pdf

The interpretation of the regulations is a simple one for a traditional package holiday or even for parts of a package sold to a customer by one organiser, eg a high-street travel agency or a web-based travel agency. In Task 5 you used separate companies to find the cheapest deal for the holiday in Majorca. Do you think that this type of booking is protected under the Package Travel Regulations? Find out more about this issue and list the advantages to the customer of being protected under these regulations. Consider also the impact of these regulations on the travel agency who is offering to book separate elements of the package. Booking separate elements of a package is called *dynamic packaging* and this is the focus of Activity 2.

ACTIVITY 2

This activity focuses on two 'hot topics': **Dynamic Packaging** and **Home-working**. Researching these two topics will enable you to appreciate and explain the complex relationships that operate in the retail and business travel environment and the impact they are having on the industry as a whole. These are current topics that have been featured and debated in many recent travel trade publications and there is wide scope for your research.

Task 1

Dynamic Packaging

The following is an extract from the Travel Technology Initiative Spring Conference 2005 publicity material:

> The hot topic of 2005 is dynamic packaging, everyone is talking about it but few can agree on what it is, why it is needed and how best to implement it.
>
> The traditionalists say it is no more than tailor-made tour operating, something the industry has been doing for as long as tour operators have existed. They claim Dynamic Packaging is no more than an established way of selling travel, dressed up in new clothes.
>
> Yet, new entrants into the industry are firm in their belief that their dynamic packaging booking engines are new, exciting and will give them a real edge. They are proud of the technology that they have developed and are even making it available to traditional travel industry players. Meanwhile, agents are not allowing themselves to be left out. They are embracing dynamic packaging as they seek to make a living in the new world of zero commission flights, bundling these with commissionable accommodation and extras. They are building their own technology and taking their fate into their own hands.
>
> Do they need their own technology? New businesses such as holidayandmore.com, lowcostbeds.com and Holiday Brokers are springing up with the specific remit to provide products that agents can dynamically package.
>
> Is dynamic packaging allowing travel agents to reposition as the tour operators of the future? Will they and the new dynamic packagers challenge the established operators' dominance of the leisure travel market? Will the tour operator system suppliers build dynamic packaging systems that will allow established tour operators to maintain their market share?
>
> There are many questions surrounding the future of dynamic packaging.

Since 2005, dynamic packaging has become well established with agents and tour operators offering the dynamic packaged product. What is dynamic packaging two years on?

Read and analyse the following articles, discuss and make notes so you can prepare to debate the concept and the impact of dynamic packaging on the retail and business travel environment.

Travel Weekly – 7 March 2007

What is dynamic packaging?

Dynamic packaging is the practice of selling holiday components separately rather than in a single package. Agents are increasingly turning to dynamic packaging to compete with the prices and flexibility offered by online retailers.

It can be a legal minefield, however, and there is potential for agents who dynamically package to find themselves in a difficult position if something goes wrong.

Travel Weekly – 8 March 2007

Opinion: Dynamic packaging is about service, not just price

Brian Young
Sales director, Holiday Brokers

Time and time again we hear price is king in the dynamic packaging market.

I've heard of agents willing to switch a sale from one supplier to another for as little as £1. I have also been quoted the acronym BOS, which stands for:

- Buy cheaper than competitors
- Operate cheaper than competitors
- Sell cheaper than competitors.

This sums up the sector perfectly.

Most frontline sales staff only care about price as they are often paid commission only and have high targets. Do they consider other key issues such as hotel quality or the operational support offered by the accommodation provider?

The answer is clearly no, with it being left to the customer services department to deal with the issues and often pay out more than the profit made in compensation.

Many retailers are now realising that although dynamic packaging is boosting their short-term profits, it may also be damaging their reputation and customer retention. So what should sensible agents be doing?

Product knowledge is key. Experience is invaluable, but technology makes it easier with most agents able to access sources such as the Gazetteers truth guides.

The simplest solution, however, is for management to drop suppliers which regularly overbook clients, do not respond to requests for assistance or have a high complaint ratio.

Unless managements give staff the right products to sell and take a wider view than price, how can they expect staff not to just sell the cheapest? Yes, price is king, but when the difference is pence, ignore price and focus on which partner gives the best service; this is key to delivering your client's holiday and the chance they will return to you next year.

As consumer-generated content grows on the internet, 'word of web' will be much more powerful than word of mouth and you will not want any bad coverage. People believe other people's reviews far more than glossy advertising or good-looking shop windows.

Travel Weekly – 2 March 2007

Opinion: Dynamic packaging has come of age

John Harding

Sales and marketing director, Hotels4u.com

This year will go down in the annals of the travel industry as the year that dynamic packaging was recognised as the way of the future for the independent sector and the vertically integrated operators.

While the independents have a clear focus on their route to market due to the realignment of the majors' distribution policies, the major operators have been unable to expand their traditional markets and have realised the way forward is to recognise the needs of the customer.

The customer is king and the retail travel trade is reacting positively to maintain its place in the distribution network.

To assist in this seismic move there is a range of tools to help agents keep ahead of the game. Customers are voting with their keyboards and driving the trade to demand even better marketing tools from software suppliers.

I've never been so optimistic for the travel sector as I am today. The innovation of those who have seen that they must adjust to the demands from the market is truly awe-inspiring and I salute them.

In all this exciting marketing activity agents should not forget that they will probably be changing their business model. They must address regulatory needs to ensure they respect the requirements of the Package Travel Regulations and the CAA, and do not fall foul of the authorities.

I would urge every agent to carry out a thorough audit of their products and procedures, especially relating to Public and Product liability insurance to make sure that their offerings and systems are properly protected.

Steve Endacott was a speaker at the TTI Spring conference in 2005 as the Chief Executive of Holiday Brokers, a division of the On Holiday Group which was created in 2003 by Steven Endacott and Bill Allen. With over 30 years' experience behind them their venture was sure to be a success, when in 2004 they were voted best, trade site only, dynamic packaging company by The British Travel Awards. Steve is responsible for moving the concept of dynamic packaging into the centre of the travel stage. Steve is currently Chief Executive of the On Holiday Group.

Check out their website for a profile of Steve:
http://www.onholidaygroup.com/steve-endacott.php

Travel Weekly – 2 March 2007

Interview: Steve Endacott on dynamic packaging

Steven Endacott is the Chief Executive of the On Holiday Group and has enjoyed a high profile career at directorship level in some of the UK's largest tour operating groups

If dynamic packaging was a living being, at what stage in its life-cycle is it currently at?

It is still in its infancy. Dynamic packaging is a natural progression from the traditional operator model. You have to be the lowest cost producer and to do that you have to drive volume for the hotelier to give you the best rates. If you get the best rates you get the volume – it is a virtuous circle.

How do you see dynamic packaging developing in the short term?

When dynamic packaging came along it was primarily accommodation-only, now the major players have added transfers, insurance and other ancillaries. My favourite word is 'co-opposition' – you have to co-operate and compete at the same time, there's no choice.

What gives dynamic packaging firms an advantage over traditional tour operators?

You have to provide the cheapest seat in the marketplace irrespective of where it comes from, so you cannot own an airline. That's why we will continue to beat traditional operators because many of them are committed to filling seats. Dynamic package tour operating is zero-risk – we do not commit to beds or seats and we are consumer focused not asset focused.

What's the recipe for a successful dynamic packaging company?

Low-cost carriers have established a model of selling cheap early on and punishing people for booking late. That means any operator wanting to work with a low-cost carrier must link to its reservation system and the package price is dictated entirely by their flight price. That's a radically aggressive model and the opposite of the big tour operators. We are driving a stake right into the heart of traditional tour operating.

Is it all about competing on price?

No, the weakness of dynamic packaging has been delivery in resort, that is why we set up Destination Care. On Holiday Group and Holiday Taxis send 750,000 people a year to overseas airports and, if we're not careful, we could be waving them goodbye. We should be waiting for them at the airport, offering car hire, currency, a table at a restaurant. Delivery of holidays is moving towards personalised service. If I was an operator I would be doubling the number of reps.

Does the merger of Thomas Cook and MyTravel herald a resurgence of traditional operators?

It will slow down change. The history of travel shows two plus two equals three. When these two giants come together you are going to have the management team distracted, they are going to cut capacity and effectively be putting a big neon sign up saying 'come and have a go'. The big tour operators have to change their models within two years or they are going to go backwards. They have the wealth, the knowledge and the people, you can't assume they won't evolve.

Do you think the public is aware of what dynamic packaging is and where they stand if something goes wrong?

As long as they get a good holiday, whether it is manufactured dynamically or with a traditional operator, they don't care. Consumers flying with low-cost carriers know a seat at that price cannot be bonded. They see bonding as being like extended warranties at Dixons. If they did want it we would give it to them. That's why Fresh Holidays is completely bonded and Holiday Brokers is unbonded.

How important is dynamic packaging for agents?

Dynamic packaging is the best thing that's ever happened to independent agents because it's complicated. The more accommodation-only providers on the web, the more complicated it becomes and successful agents will become experts in web tools and do the work for the consumer. But that is not going to be done sitting behind a desk in a high-street shop. The future is community-based retailing – getting off your backside and going to the consumer.

One month on from this article comes the news of the big four mergers to create the big two. Note the comments of Steve Endacott in relation to dynamic packaging.

Travel Trade Gazette – 29 March 2007

Analysis: New travel groups must adapt to survive

The speed with which travel's big four announced mergers to create a big two has prompted some cataclysmic language over the last couple of months.

After the original Thomas Cook/MyTravel deal a Travel Counsellors' recruitment advertisement likened such giants of the travel industry to dinosaurs, and chairman David Speakman drew on Charles Darwin when he said: 'It's not the strongest of the species that survive, nor the most intelligent. It's the most responsive to change. Is Thomas Cook changing or just getting bigger?'

Shock to the system

Building on the theme, On Holiday Group chief executive Steve Endacott compared last week's surprise revelation of a TUI/First Choice merger to a meteor hitting the earth.

The question is, which species of travel company will this meteor wipe out, and can the lumbering giants, whose position some consider to be precarious, compete with smaller, quicker challengers that look increasingly able to run rings around them?

Conceding that it was these voracious young upstarts who were taking market share from the big players, First Choice chief executive Peter Long explained the background to the decision to join the race for consolidation last week.

It was, he said, these companies and the dynamic packaging environment they have spawned that has forced consolidation, and their impact will also be used to justify a big two to the competition authorities.

'The industry map has changed significantly over the last five years, and will change again, and if you do not adapt all you will do is shrink,' said Long.

'You have numerous tour operators within the traditional sector, you have the big four and then you have what's going on outside of us like the low-cost airlines, which have taken a huge amount of business from us, firstly with flight-only then with dynamic packaging.'

In what turned out to be a prescient comment, given announcements this week from Ryanair and easyJet about enhancing their online holiday products, he added: 'easyJet already offers hotels so you can component-build and Ryanair is already looking to come into that space. These are well-financed businesses. easyJet is about to become a FTSE 100 company and Ryanair is even bigger.'

Long's view of how the new TUI Travel Group he is set to run will become fit for the future is simple – it comes down to those eternal business objectives of margins, profitability and efficiency.

'You have to be efficient because that is the only way to compete against the whole cross section of different competitors,' he said.

'Are we going to increase prices? Absolutely not. Even if we did the consumer would not buy it. The only thing you have to ensure is you run your business in the most efficient way. Consumers demand value, that's the world we live in.'

Increasing margins

Long's success in driving up margins at First Choice towards the magical 5% has been matched by the efforts of Thomas Cook UK chief executive Manny Fontenla-Novoa, but Thomson survives on just 2% and MyTravel has only just broken even in the UK.

The end of skinny margins will be a priority for Long in his new position at the helm of what will become Europe's largest tour operator and, like the merged Thomas Cook/MyTravel, a FTSE 100 company in its own right.

'The opportunity we have now is to improve margins. Clearly, large-scale businesses that are on very low margins are a high risk from an investment perspective.

'TUI has made significant investments in its infrastructure and has a number of plans which will result in those investments showing increased returns. There is a big prize for us there.'

One of the major worries for the big four will be that while the work goes on to bring their operations together and while thousands of employees fret over their future job, the day-to-day running of the business suffers.

However, speaking to *Travel Weekly* at the beginning of our Dynamic Packaging Month, even Endacott, that most vocal champion of dynamic packaging, refused to rule out the possibility of the big four, or the big two as they may soon be known, adapting to survive.

'The traditional tour operators have the wealth and the knowledge and the people and you cannot assume for a second that they won't evolve,' he said.

'You dynamically package and survive or you don't and you die. It really is like that. The big operators are going to get it and if you are an independent agency you have absolutely no choice. I would say that – but I think it's getting more and more true by the day.'

Task 2

There are many more articles and news items about dynamic packaging; you should conduct research and build a file on this topic. As a group, debate the following questions:

- Is dynamic packaging a new concept, or has it been around as tailor-made holidays for years?
- Is the package holiday a product of the past?
- How will the retail and business travel agent adapt to compete with the new dynamic packaging companies?

You should produce a summary sheet, showing the main conclusions from your discussions for each debate.

Task 3

Home-working

The other concept that has grown in stature over the last few years is home-working. One of the pioneers of home-working in the travel industry in the UK is David Speakman, Chairman and Founder of Travel Counsellors Plc. The following extracts are taken from a recent report written by the company's Group Managing Director, Steve Byrne:

What is Home-working?

There is no one simple model for home-working. There is no such thing as a common or standard or typical home-working company. Home-working companies work in different ways. In the past, some have had call centres, with calls generated by advertising on the television or the Internet. Many of those companies are now closing their call centres and the employees now work from home. Other home-working companies advertise on Teletext and other media, and use home-based agents to field those calls.

The Growth of Home-working

Given the growth of home-working in Europe and America, it is a sector to be taken seriously. In the UK, there are approximately 25,000 travel agencies working in conventional high street shops and around 2,000 home-based travel professionals, and it is a sector that is growing quickly.

The most mature home-based market in the world is in America where there are over 40,000 professional home-based agents. It is forecast that there will be nearly 300,000 there within 3–5 years.

Home-working provides a cost-effective way to communicate and distribute your product. Home-based agents are technically very knowledgeable and astute. They are used to dealing with the Internet and searching for information. Home-working companies such as Travel Counsellors have set up systems to communicate to their agents whilst they work at home. Companies support their staff by providing them with updates and online training.

To date, home-working has not hugely impacted on the distribution of the product in the UK but it is a fast growing market.

Recognition of Home-working

Over the past 2 to 3 years, the concept of travel agents working from home has been established as a professional vehicle through which people can arrange and sell their holidays. In June 2007 Travel Counsellors, a home-working company, won a consumer award for the UK Best Travel Agency. Home-working agencies survive purely based on the power of the service they provide their customers, so they have to have an emotional attachment with the customer. This is why the repeat business for these companies is very high, over 60%.

Summary

This is a fast growing market with new entrants all the time. Home-working is already impacting on the distribution of the travel product.

The above is a PDF file from the following web address: http://www.spain.info/NR/rdonlyres/A3BE769F-EE06-437A-9656-C0052E09E3CD/0/Homeworking.pdf

List the companies who offer a home-working service in the UK.

Select one of these companies and prepare a presentation to the rest of the group and within the presentation answer the following questions:

- Who owns it?
- When did it start to operate?
- Where does it operate?
- What are the requirements to be a home-worker?
- What benefits does it offer the home-workers?
- What are the benefits to the customer?
- What are the benefits to the company?

Here are some articles from *Travel Weekly* to help you in your research:

Travel Weekly – 27 July 2006

No regrets about home-working, say Travel Counsellors

A MASSIVE 98% of Travel Counsellors home-workers claim they wouldn't return to the high street.

The figure, from the company's annual home-worker survey, has increased from 96% in 2005.

An overwhelming 95% of Personal Counsellors claim they are happier now than in their previous job, citing a number of reasons, including no commuting, flexible hours and more free time.

Nearly all (97%) of the 541 Travel Counsellors polled said they would recommend the organisation to high-street agents.

Travel Counsellors support, including head office, the weekly webcast, the annual conference and business development meetings, were all rated as good or excellent by nine out of 10 home-workers.

All polled rated the company's technology as good or excellent.

Managing director Steve Byrne said the high level of support has led to a home-worker retention rate of more than 90%, in an industry which has an average staff turnover rate of around 30%.

'Despite expanding the company rapidly we have made an effort not to neglect our existing Travel Counsellors,' he said.

The typical Travel Counsellor is female, a former agency owner or manager with an average 18 years' experience. Almost a quarter (23%) have children under five years old.

Meanwhile, two-thirds revealed they are earning more money thanks to the organisation's in-house dynamic packaging system Phenix, with a further 6% saying their earnings have remained the same but would have reduced without the system.

Dynamic packaging now accounts for 22% of all Travel Counsellors' bookings.

Travel Weekly (27 July 2006) says:

There's no place like home

The homeworking phenomenon gathers pace with the major players upping the ante in the battle to get new recruits to join their businesses.

But it is not surprising more and more travel consultants are looking to go down the homeworking route when you consider the job approval ratings that homeworking companies are getting.

Figures released exclusively this week by Travel Counsellors to Travel Weekly reveal an incredible 98% of its consultants do not wish to return to the high street.

A crucial factor in this appears to be the 85% of consultants who said their work/life balance had improved since working from home – and who can say that about their own jobs in recent years?

The ability to spread your workload over any given day, evening or weekend; and the option, particularly for women, of working while bringing up children is proving a winning formula.

What's more, the intranet systems of the leading homeworking players means working from home doesn't mean working in isolation.

In fact the daily support, be it online or over the phone, is arguably more than you might receive in the office.

All this is no doubt helping the major homeworking companies to buck market trends and report significant sales growth.

So it's not just travel consultants who like the homeworking concept but their customers too.

ACTIVITY 3

In undertaking the previous activities you will have assimilated a good knowledge of the retail and business travel environment. You should now be able to evaluate the effectiveness of retail and business travel organisations and how they operate in the travel environment.

Task 1

In groups, try to illustrate the retail travel industry today from the customer's perspective. Create a series of diagrams that explain to customers the options available to them when booking a holiday. Try and illustrate the relationships between the different organisations.

Task 2

In groups, try to illustrate the business travel industry today. Create a diagram to show the different booking options available to a local business for business travel.

Task 3

Select one company from the list below and prepare a presentation to the group to show that this company has been particularly effective in its operations in the current retail and/or business travel climate. Justify why you think this company has been successful.

- easyJet
- Jet2
- Travel Counsellors
- On Holiday
- A local retail or business agency of your choice
- First Choice
- Dial A Flight
- Hotelopia.

Hopefully this research will have helped you to make some decisions with regard to your future employment in this dynamic industry and helped you to form some opinions about the industry itself. You should report these within your presentation.

In summary

Your findings should have led you towards gaining an in-depth understanding of the complex nature of the retail and business travel environment. You will probably have been surprised by the inter-relationships and inter-dependencies of the organisations involved, and the need to be open to change in order to succeed in this competitive and volatile market.

A good example is the dynamic packaging company On Holiday Group, formed in 2004 in direct response to evolving markets and advances in technology. You can read about this company on their website:

http://www.onholidaygroup.com/steve-endacott.php

You will find that they have now linked with Jet2, a low-cost scheduled airline based out of Leeds Bradford airport, to offer package holidays, hotels and other products and services and so advancing the growth of yet another Internet holiday company.

So, how will you book your holiday this year and in the future? Will you be one of those who are happy to put themselves in the hands of the high-street travel agent? Or are you now much more knowledgeable and keen to put together your own package by visiting the websites of a range of travel providers and dynamic-packaging companies? Whatever you do in the future, you are now much more aware of the booking options available.

You will perhaps have made some decisions along the way with regard to your future employment in this exciting industry and perhaps reviewed your original career aspirations in the light of your findings in Unit 9.

You will perhaps have made some decisions along the way with regard to your future employment in this exciting industry and perhaps reviewed your original career aspirations in the light of your findings in Unit 9.

MARKED ASSIGNMENTS

UNIT 12 – TOUR OPERATIONS

Sample Assignment
Unit 12 – Tour Operations

This assignment is providing work that will allow you to achieve grading criteria P2, M2 and D2.

Scenario

You are working for a medium-sized tour operator and have decided to apply for an internal vacancy in the product-development department.

To assess your suitability for this dynamic and challenging department, the product-development manager has asked you to carry out some detailed research into different categories of tour operator and to produce an up-to-date, factual report with your findings.

Task 1

Your first task is to examine the products and services offered by different categories of tour operator.

1.1 You should start by explaining what is meant by the following types of tour operator:

- Outbound
- Inbound
- Domestic
- Independent
- Specialist

Guidelines: You should provide at least three examples of tour operators within each category.

1.2 Describe the products and services provided by different categories of tour operator including:

- Components of a standard package
- Tailor-made options available
- Range of destinations
- Accommodation choices
- Transport options
- Ancillary products and services
- Target markets

Guidelines: You must select one tour operator from each category for this task, making a total of five descriptions of products and services. You could produce separate information files for each tour operator if you wish.

Tasks 1.1 and 1.2 will together provide evidence for P2.

Task 2

The product-development manager would like to see if you are also capable of more in-depth research and has asked you to make a presentation on a selected tour operator's products and services. You can select a tour operator of your choice and analyse how its portfolio of products and services meets the needs of its target market(s).

Guidelines: You will need to clearly identify the needs of the target market(s) and then show the extent to which the current range of products and services meets those needs. Make sure you give plenty of examples to support your analysis.

Task 2 will provide evidence for M2.

Task 3

Finally, to enable the product-development manager to see your potential as a member of the product-development team, you have been asked to recommend, with justification, how a selected tour operator could expand its range of products and services for its current target market or adapt its range of products and services to appeal to a new market. Submit written recommendations for consideration and justify your recommendations.

Guidelines: you must review the product range and make recommendations for how it could be expanded to widen its appeal. Make sure you justify your recommendations.

Task 3 will provide evidence for D2.

You need to produce the following:

- For P2, a report describing the products and services provided by different categories of tour operator
- For M2, a presentation with an analysis of the products and services provided by one selected tour operator
- For D2, justified proposals for how a selected tour operator could expand its range of products and services
- A comprehensive bibliography
- A learner declaration confirming that this is your own work

Suggested resources:

Dale – *BTEC National Travel and Tourism* (Heinemann, 2007)
978 0 435 44588 1

Woodhouse et al – *BTEC National Travel and Tourism* (Hodder Education, 2007)
978 0 340 94573 5

Various – *BTEC National Travel and Tourism* (Longman, 2007)
978 1 405 86807 5

Tour operator brochures

Websites. Most tour operators' websites can be located via Google.

www.ukinbound.co.uk

www.aito.co.uk

PASS LEVEL ANSWER

Unit 12 – Tour Operations Assignment Task 1

P2 describe the products and services provided by different categories of tour operator

The UK tour operating sector has hundreds of different tour operators providing holidays to meet the needs of virtually all types of customer. The main categories are:

- Outbound
- Inbound
- Domestic
- Independent
- Specialist

Outbound

Outbound tour operators organise holidays overseas for holidaymakers from the UK travelling to other countries around the world. There are hundreds of different outbound tour operators, for example:

- **First Choice Holidays** operates package holidays to Europe and beyond

- **Balkan Holidays** operates holidays to Bulgaria, Croatia, Slovenia, Montenegro, Albania, Romania and Turkey

- **Cosmos** operates touring holidays in Europe and beyond as Cosmos Tourama and package holidays mainly to holiday destinations in Europe and the USA.

Inbound

Inbound tour operators organise holidays in the UK for visitors from different countries. For example they might advertise UK holidays in the USA, Japan or France. This is much easier to do now with the internet. When the holidaymakers arrive in the UK, the inbound tour operator can arrange to meet them at the airport and provide their holiday arrangements. This could be, for example, a tour of the UK or a short stay in London. Many inbound tour operators are members of UKInbound, including:

- **All European Travel** was established in 1990 and is now one of the UK's leading Inbound Tour Operators

- **European Travel Services** was established in 1987. They provide accommodation and all other ancillary services throughout Great Britain for both individuals and groups.

- **Evan Evans Tours** started as a sightseeing company and now offers day and overnight coach and rail tours for inbound visitors to the main visitor attractions in and around London.

Domestic

Domestic tour operators organise UK holidays for people living in the UK. Many domestic tour operators also provide outbound holidays.

- **WA Shearings** was created as a result of the merger between Shearings Holidays and Wallace Arnold in March 2005. Although they also offer outbound holidays, they are best known as a domestic tour operator offering coach tours for more mature customers.

- **Grand UK** is a coach tour operator offering many domestic coach tours for people aged over 55.

- **Superbreak Mini Holidays** concentrates on the short break holiday market, mainly for the UK domestic market.

Independent

Independent tour operators are those that are independent of the large integrated companies. Many of them will belong to AITO, the Association of Independent Tour Operators. Many independent tour operators are also specialist operators (see below) and some are very small. Many independent tour operators are direct sell.

It is sometimes difficult for an independent tour operator to have their brochures stocked by large integrated travel agencies, and many of them will therefore use independent travel agents to sell their products as these agents can often give a more specialised and unbiased service.

Some examples of independent tour operators are:

- **Kirker Holidays** was established in 1986 and say that 'our aim has been to provide discerning travellers with a carefully selected range of hotels combined with private transfers, private tours and well-researched itineraries that enable you to make the most of your budget and the time that you have available' (http://www.kirkerholidays.com/)

- **Cox & Kings** claims to be one of the most experienced independent tour operators. They offer high-quality group tours and tailor-made itineraries. They say 'Our holidays range from the luxurious to the adventurous, and are planned by experts with a passion for travel and made real by dedicated staff on the ground'. (http://www.coxandkings. co.uk/)

- **Eurocamp** claims to be the market-leader in self catering holidays to Europe. They are a direct-sell independent operator.

Specialist

A specialist tour operator is one that specialises in a particular type of holiday or target group. There are a surprising number of specialist tour

119

operators based in the UK and hundreds of different specialisms, for example:

- **SAGA Holidays** – a specialist by age
- **Gambia Experience** – a specialist by destination
- **Cycling for Softies** – a specialist by activity
- **Holts Battlefield Tours** – a special interest tour operator
- **Great Rail Journeys** – a specialist by accommodation type

Some tour operators can belong to several different categories, for example an independent tour operator will also be either an inbound, domestic or outbound tour operator and could also be a specialist tour operator.

On the following pages are some profiles of tour operators in different categories describing products and services that they provide for their target markets.

✓ This provides part evidence for P2 (three examples of each category). I have written fuller notes on the feedback sheet for this task.

Club 18 –30	
Category	Club 18–30 is an example of a **specialist** tour operator; they are also outbound because they offer holidays outside the UK to holidaymakers belonging to a specific age group. Club 18–30 is part of the Thomas Cook group of companies, so they are also an integrated tour operator.
Target market	Club 18–30's target market is the youth market. Despite the name, you have to be between the ages of 17 and 35 to take one of their holidays. The holidays target people who want to 'party 24/7' or chill out on the beach by day and have a really lively nightlife. Groups are also targeted with free places offered, as many as 1 free place in 6 in early and late season, reducing to 1 free place in 18 during the July and August peak.
Range of destinations	Club 18–30 chooses its destinations for their combination of nightlife and beaches. In 2007 they featured resorts on the islands of: • Ibiza • Mallorca • Crete • Zante • Corfu • Rhodes • Cyprus • Kos • Tenerife • Gran Canaria And also Bulgaria.

Club 18−30 − CONTINUED	
Accommodation choices	Club 18−30 have their own accommodation ratings, a 'C' rating, ranging from C to CCCCC (although there is no CCCC or CCCCC accommodation in the brochure). Accommodation is said to be clean and comfortable and location is important, especially being close to the beach, the nightlife and the town. Most of the accommodation is in studios or apartments of between C and CCC standard, with private facilities, balcony and kitchenettes. Some of the accommodation has air conditioning, most has a swimming pool and a pool bar. Resorts like Sunny Beach in Bulgaria also offer CCC standard hotels, which have more facilities available.
Transport options	All standard packages include charter flights mainly with Thomas Cook from a total of 14 UK airports in 2007. In-flight meals are not included in the holiday price. You can also make flexible arrangements where you have a choice of charter, scheduled and no-frills carriers (e.g. easyJet) but you have to pay in full at the time of booking when you book a flexible trip with anything other than a charter.
Ancillary products and services	Travel insurance is compulsory and Club 18−30 recommends insurance cover with AXA Insurance UK Ltd, with varying prices, for example £23.99 for 10-17 days. A full 'rep' service is included at the resort. A wide variety of optional excursions is offered in the resort. When staying in Ibiza and Mallorca, free club tickets are offered for nightclub opening and closing parties when staying at selected accommodations on selected dates. Discounted tickets are available at many other destinations. Club 18−30 offers pre-bookable flight services: • For an additional £20 per person friends can pre-book their flight seats together • For an additional £50 per person each way you can book extra leg room • For £12 per person return you can book in-flight meals Club 18−30 can organise airport car parking at competitive rates with BCP at 21 UK airports, from £2.99 per day. They also book UK airport hotels.
A standard package	A typical Club 18−30 holiday is a package to Rhodes. The 2007 brochure features eight choices of studio and apartment accommodation in Faliaraki. Faliaraki has a beach over one mile long with lots of water sports on offer and there is a great nightlife too. The price includes: • Return charter flights – you can choose from six UK airports to Rhodes using either Thomas Cook Airways or First Choice Airways, paying a supplement to travel from London Gatwick, Manchester, Stansted, Liverpool and Glasgow. There is no supplement from Birmingham. • Air Passenger Duty and taxes • Free luggage allowance of 20kg

121

Club 18-30 – CONTINUED	
	• Airport transfers (except late bookings) • Accommodation on a room only basis, with simple self catering facilities • The services of Club reps. The accommodation in Rhodes is of CC and CCC standard. The CCC+ Millennium Studios are typical, with pool, 24 hour bar with TV, snacks available all day, friendly atmosphere. Studios sleep 2-3 and have kitchenette, private facilities, air conditioning (payable locally) and balcony or terrace. Prices at the Millennium Studios vary from £335 to £549 for 7 nights or £369 to £635 for 14 nights. To make the holiday more enjoyable there are lots of optional day trips and night trips that can be booked through the reps in the resort.
Tailor made	Although most of the holidays in the brochure are for 7 or 14 nights, Club 18–30 allows you to '*Remix it your own way*', selecting dates, duration, airport and combining these with Club 18–30 accommodation, having the services of their reps, excursions, etc. These flexible trips are available in Ibiza, Mallorca, Gran Canaria and Tenerife and they are fully bonded with ABTA and ATOL so holidaymakers have all the protection of a normal package holiday. A choice of charter, scheduled and low cost airlines are offered on the flexible programme.

✓ This provides part evidence for P2 (specialist and outbound). I have written fuller notes on the feedback sheet for this task.

Superbreak Mini Holidays	
Category	Superbreak Mini Holidays Ltd is predominantly a **domestic** tour operator offering short break holidays in the UK. They are the market leader for UK short breaks and are part of Holidaybreak plc. They have several domestic holiday brochures including UK Hotel Short Breaks, Luxury Hotel Collection, and Theme Park and Attraction Breaks. There is also a dedicated brochure for short breaks in London.
Target market	Superbreak targets different markets in the UK. Their main target market is individuals (i.e. singles, couples, etc) on leisure breaks. Many themed breaks are offered to appeal to different types of leisure customer. These include Murder Mystery Weekends, Spa breaks, Theatre and entertainment breaks. They also have a specialist group department to organise stag and hen parties, theatre breaks, golf breaks, school groups and conferences. They also target families and advertise some breaks where children under 16 can stay and travel free.

Superbreak Mini Holidays – CONTINUED

Range of destinations	London is the main destination featured by Superbreak and there is a special brochure called London Travel Service. The short break brochure includes 400 key locations in the UK including cities like York, Oxford and Glasgow, scenic locations like the Cotswolds and the Lake District and coastal resorts like Blackpool, Torquay and Brighton. The Theme Park and Attractions brochure includes breaks featuring Alton Towers, Legoland and Blackpool Pleasure Beach and it is also possible to add tickets for top attractions and castles across the country including the London Eye and Warwick Castle.
Accommodation choices	Superbreak offers over 1000 2- to 5-star hotels in the UK so there is something to meet most tastes and budgets. For example in London you could choose the famous 5- star Savoy Hotel, the 4-star K West & Spa, the 3-star Travelodge in London's Docklands or the 2-star Regent Palace Hotel in Piccadilly Circus. In the rest of the UK hotels vary from Travelodge up to 5- star hotels like the Balmoral in Edinburgh and the Lowry in Manchester. Hotels vary in size, style and facilities and include independent hotels as well as those that are part of a chain or franchise, e.g. Best Western, Holiday Inn and Sheraton. The advertised board basis is usually bed and breakfast although dinner can be added at many hotels for a supplement. It is also possible to pay a supplement to upgrade accommodation at many hotels.
Transport options	The advertised prices don't include travel, however Superbreak can offer rail inclusive breaks to all mainline stations in the UK, for example with Virgin Trains, GNER and Midland Mainline. The routes are coded and there is a set price for standard and first class travel from each area code to the destination. For example, to travel from York to Edinburgh with GNER would cost £26 standard class and £89 first class return in the 2007 brochure. It is possible to book day trips on the Orient Express.
Ancillary products and services	Superbreak offers a wide range of ancillary products and services: • low cost travel insurance for £5.95 per person on domestic breaks • London discount vouchers are provided free with every booking to London • All holidays include one year's membership to Days Out UK • Activity packages with 'Activity Superstore' can be added to holidays at many locations, e.g. a helicopter flight, white-water rafting and a Ferrari challenge • Stag and hen breaks can include paintballing, quad biking, spa packages, Comedy Club and rock climbing

Superbreak Mini Holidays – CONTINUED	
	• Private dining can be arranged • London and other city sightseeing passes can be purchased e.g. hop on hop off buses • Entry tickets to attractions are offered e.g. London Eye, Madame Tussauds • Packages can include city tours, boat trips, events such as the Clothes Show, Chelsea Flower Show, International Horse Show • Theatre tickets and theatre dinners are offered • Gift vouchers
A standard package	A standard spa package at the Runnymede Hotel and Spa. This is a 4-star privately owned hotel in Surrey set in 12 acres of gardens. The break will include: • 2 nights' bed and breakfast in the hotel with full English breakfast • A Prescription Facial (1 hour) to leave skin radiant and revitalized. • Back massage (1/2 hour) Guests can use all of the spa and leisure facilities in the hotel including: • 18m indoor pool • whirlpool bath • sauna • steam room • outdoor tennis courts • gymnasium and aerobics studio The two night package costs £230 per person and there is a supplement of £50 on Mondays to Thursdays. It is possible to upgrade to an Executive Room for £20 per person. The prices are based on two people sharing a twin or double room. You have to be over 18 years of age to book the spa package. Rail travel can be arranged if required.
Tailor made	Customers tailor make their own short break with Superbreak by selecting dates, accommodation to suit their budget and they have the option to select rail travel and a wide variety of leisure, activity and entertainment packages.

Eurocamp	
Category	I am using Eurocamp as my example of an **independent** tour operator. However they are also **outbound** and **specialist** as they specialise in self catering camping and mobile home holidays in Europe. Eurocamp is part of Holidaybreak plc and is a member of AITO and ABTA.

✓ This provides part evidence for P2 (domestic and specialist). I have written fuller notes on the feedback sheet for this task.

Eurocamp – CONTINUED

Target market	Eurocamp mainly targets families. Children travel free and they offer many facilities for children including kids clubs at many of their holiday parks. The company has won awards for its parent friendly family holidays. However they also target couples and older people, particularly outside the school holidays. This will help them to have greater occupancy levels at these times. In 2008 you can even take your dog! www.eurocamp.co.uk 
Range of destinations	In 2007 Eurocamp featured 150 campsites in Europe including the Vendee, Brittany, Dordogne, Loire, Alps, Jura and Corsica in France, Lake Garda, Tuscany, Sardinia and Elba in Italy, Germany, Holland, Switzerland, Austria, Croatia and the Costa Brava and Costa Verde in Spain. Appendix 1 shows a map with the range of destinations offered in 2007.
Accommodation choices	You can choose from tents, chalets and mobile home accommodation. The cheapest type of accommodation offered by Eurocamp is a fully equipped tent: *All our tents are made to a very high standard and come complete with a parasol and sunloungers, plus everything you need for cooking, eating and relaxing (including a barbecue where they are permitted).*www.eurocamp.co.uk Next you have six different levels of mobile home and chalet accommodation ranging from Grade 1 (top of the range) to Grade 6. The Monaco Deluxe is Grade 1: **10m × 3.5m** *This first class accommodation has everything you could possibly need for the perfect holiday and is ideal for those who enjoy the finer things in life. The modern kitchen has contemporary stainless steel appliances. There is a spacious living interior and three impressively big bedrooms – the master being en-suite to the main bathroom. All these features make the Monaco Deluxe a real luxury experience.* www.eurocamp.co.uk The Cezanne is an example of Grade 6: **8m × 3m** *With bedrooms at each end of the mobile home, the children get independence and the parents get privacy. No supplements apply to this model making it great value for money.* www.eurocamp.co.uk You pay more for newer and larger accommodation, built to a higher specification.

125

Eurocamp – CONTINUED	
Transport options	Most people taking Eurocamp holidays travel in their own cars. Holiday prices include a mid week channel crossing from Dover to Calais with P & O ferries. There are other options where you pay a supplement, for example: • Weekend crossings • Channel tunnel • Sea France from Dover to Calais • Brittany Ferries from Plymouth to Roscoff • P & O North Sea Ferries from Hull to Rotterdam or Zeebrugge Most holiday makers would then drive from the channel port to their holiday park. Eurocamp can organise en route hotel or holiday park accommodation for long journeys and they also provide maps and route planning. As low cost flights have expanded, Eurocamp now offers flights to many destinations and they can organise a taxi transfer to the holiday park, as well as airport car parking in the UK. Motorail is another transport option to save people from having to drive long distances to the south of France and Italy.
Ancillary products and services	As already stated Eurocamp can organise overnight accommodation in hotels or holiday parks, route planning, airport car parking and taxi transfers. All holidaymakers must be insured and Eurocamp offers insurance with Voyager Insurance Services and underwritten by Europ Assistance. They offer personal individual, couple or family insurance and vehicle insurance including overseas breakdown cover. Additional products and services offered by Eurocamp are: • The services of holiday representatives • Children's clubs on many parks • Activity tents (additional charge) • Linen hire • Buggies, stair gates, high chairs and other services for young children.
A standard package	A typical package for a family with two primary school aged children travelling by car from Kent to stay for 7 nights in August in a mobile home on a holiday park in Northern France with lots of activities for the children: A suitable holiday park would be La Croix du Vieux Pont near Paris. Eurocamp says: *It's ideal for children thanks to a special parkland play area, as well as three lovely pools, one with a retractable roof and one with a waterslide. These are overlooked by the pleasant terrace bar and restaurant/take-away, which are attractively housed in rustic farm buildings. There is also a beauty therapy and gym centre where you can take advantage of the services of qualified professionals.* www.eurocamp.co.uk

Eurocamp – CONTINUED	
	If they travel mid week, the holiday price includes ferry crossing for car plus up to 6 occupants from Dover to Calais with P & O ferries. They can choose the time of day that they travel. They can choose an alternative route, an alternative operator, or to travel on a weekend at a supplement. If they prefer, Eurocamp could organise flights to Paris.
	At the holiday park there are Eurocamp Fun Stations (children's clubs) for aged 4 plus and 7 plus where the children can join in daily activities. The family will have the services of Eurocamp representatives and babysitting is available. In addition the park is set beside a lake and pedaloes can be hired.
	They could stay in a Verona mobile home which Eurocamp describes as:
	The Verona, with its open contemporary interior and spacious kitchen, is one of our most popular mobile homes and is ideal for young families. There are two versions of this model; one has a central living area and the other has an end living area. Both have patio doors and there is plenty of room for all your holiday knick-knacks. Please note that blankets and pillows are provided but you will be required to take sheets and pillow cases. www.eurocamp.co.uk
	The kitchen is fully equipped and in addition linen and charcoal barbecues can be hired. Larger mobile homes are available, as are tents.
	There is a shop on site and takeaway and restaurant facilities if they don't want to self-cater.
	As the park is near to Disneyland Paris, Eurocamp can also organise entrance tickets if required.
	This holiday costs £950 for the whole family on 18 August 2007.
Tailor made	All of Eurocamp's holidays are tailor made in that you put together your own package with as many nights as you want (subject to availability), in as many campsites as you want, with a choice of accommodation types and methods of transport.
	It is unlikely that any two holidays would be exactly the same as customers have total flexibility to go 'Park Hopping' and to self-drive using a variety of ferry options or fly to many destinations.

Cosmos	
Category	I am using Cosmos as an example of an **outbound** tour operator. They also claim to be the largest UK independent tour operator. The Cosmos group of companies has its own airline (Monarch), touring holidays (Cosmos Tourama and Globus Gateway) and accommodation provider (somewhertostay.com). AVRO Holidays, a charter tour operator is also part of the Cosmos group.

127

✓ This provides part evidence for P2 (independent, specialist and outbound). Again, I have written fuller notes on the feedback sheet for this task.

Cosmos – CONTINUED	
Target market	Cosmos aims to have something for everyone. Their summer sun brochure targets mainly families and groups. Families are also well-catered for with brochures for Florida and Lapland, whereas honeymooners and couples might be attracted by the Distant Dreams brochure. They also have a specialist Weddings brochure. Cosmos Tourama is also sold overseas so there are many different nationalities on these tours including British, American, Japanese, Australian, etc.
Range of destinations	In 2007 Cosmos has separate brochures offering holidays to: • Spain and Portugal • Turkey and Bulgaria • Florida • Lapland • America, Canada, Europe and Worldwide (Tourama) • Greece and Cyprus • Virginia • River Cruises • Croatia, Italy, Malta and North Africa They have an extensive portfolio of destinations. Their top ten destination in 2007 are: • Majorca • Florida • Portugal • Egypt • Costa del Sol • Turkey • Maldives • Rhodes • Italy • Kenya
Accommodation choices	Accommodation varies according to the brochure. For example there is a special villas with pools brochure which offers a wide range of good quality villa accommodation. In the Mediterranean, Cosmos offers mainly 3- and 4-star accommodation in hotels and self catering, but they also have an 'Elite' range of 5-star accommodation. Cosmos apply their own grading system of diamonds.
Transport options	Where possible Cosmos uses its own airline, Monarch Airlines, and they fly from several UK airports, including Gatwick, Manchester, Birmingham and Glasgow. On arrival they offer coach or taxi transfers to the resort. Cosmos Tourama coach tours use Cosmos liveried coaches with air conditioning and all the comforts people would expect on a long coach tour.

Cosmos – CONTINUED	
Ancillary products and services	Cosmos sells insurance with Rock Insurance Services Limited. When using Monarch Airlines, customers can pre-book seats from £7 per person and pay extra for Monarch plus, VIP airport lounges (£13 per person) and airport parking with BCP, from £3 per day. In flight meals are not included but can be booked for £12 per person. Airport accommodation is available via FHR at 19 airport hotels. You can book National Express travel to your airport. A wide range of optional excursions is made available to holidaymakers in resort and on coach tours. Car Rental is available with Sixt Rent a car. You can book tee off times for golf holidays with 3D tee times and even purchase E Kit phone cards offering a 70% reduction in phone charges. Extras can be arranged in resort, including welcome packs, special celebrations, late check-out rooms and kids beach packs.
A standard package	A typical standard package with Cosmos to the Hotel Royal Bay in Elenite Beach in Bulgaria in 2007 includes: • Choice of flights to Bourgas Airport from London Gatwick, Manchester or Birmingham, with nil supplement from Gatwick and between £25 and £45 supplement from Manchester or Birmingham • Coach transfer to resort • Services of a Cosmos representative • Accommodation in a hotel room sleeping two adults and two children (double sofa bed) with private facilities, balcony or terrace, sea view and air conditioning • Use of all hotel facilities including swimming pools, parasols • Evening entertainment • Full board with buffet breakfast and lunch, buffet or a la carte dinner, free snacks from the pavilion • All locally produced beers, wine, spirits and soft drinks • Use of tennis courts, table tennis, windsurfing, minigolf, pedaloes and mountain bikes The only extras are for a return taxi transfer (£28 return) and single rooms at £8 per night. This holiday in August 2007 costs from £495 to £555 per adult and £249 per child.
Tailor made	Cosmos offer 'FlexiStays' holidays because they know that not everyone wants to be tied to a one or two week break. With 'FlexiStays' people can choose which day of the week they travel and how long they stay for. They include scheduled flights and accommodation, but do not include transfers. Taxi transfers can be organised at additional charges. These holidays are sold mainly via the internet. You can also put together your own package by using Cosmos' airline, Monarch and their web based accommodation company somewheretostay.com.

129

✓ This provides part evidence for P2 (outbound). I have written fuller notes on the feedback sheet for this task.

Evan Evans Tours	
Category	Evan Evans Tours started as a sightseeing company over 70 years ago. They have since developed and are now also an **inbound** tour operator and a member of UKInbound.
Target market	Evan Evans Tours target inbound holidaymakers who use London as a base for part of their UK holiday. These include a wide range of nationalities but the Japanese are amongst their biggest customers and Japanese language tours are offered daily to Stonehenge, Bath, Windsor, Stratford, Warwick, Leeds Castle and Canterbury. Japanese visitors are also attracted to tours, for example the Lake District (Beatrix Potter) and Liverpool (the Beatles). Americans are attracted to historic and cultural destinations like Bath, Stonehenge, York and Edinburgh.
Range of destinations	The main tours take place in and around London. These are day trips organized for people staying in London hotels for example: • Stonehenge • Windsor • Bath • Oxford However the company can also organise longer tours to: • Edinburgh • The Lake District, which is billed as 'Beatrix Potter' country; • Liverpool and the Beatles • Tours of Britain including Cambridge, York, Edinburgh, Chester and Stratford Upon Avon
Accommodation choices	Evan Evans Tours uses European Travel Services to offer discount rates at more than 100 London Hotels. They can provide accommodation to suit all budgets from 1 star to 5 stars. Of 193 hotels used in London in 2007, 5 are 1-star; 20 are 2-star; 84 are 3-star; 55 are 4-star and 15 are 5-star.
Transport options	Top of the range coaches are used for tours and transfers, with air conditioning. Coaches have Evan Evans Tours livery. Some tours are organised by train. For example to Edinburgh: • Round-trip train tickets to Edinburgh with reserved seats • Hop-on hop-off Sightseeing tour of Edinburgh • Tour of the Highlands – see Urquhart Castle • Panoramic tour of Inverness • visit Pitlochry • A free city map and information booklet
Ancillary products and services	Evan Evans Tours offers: • day trips to London attractions • a comprehensive courtesy pick-up service from or near London hotels • inbound or outbound airport to hotel transfers • theatre tickets • hotel to theatre transfers

Evan Evans Tours – CONTINUED	
	• on tour they can offer extras for example a pub lunch or traditional afternoon tea • representatives at Victoria Coach station where morning tours depart at 0845 • drop off at London hotels at the end of the day • the services of professional Blue badge London guides
A standard package	Evan Evans Tours offer several standard tours of Britain. These are of a short duration because many inbound visitors are working to a tight schedule and might also be visiting Europe too. A typical four day tour of Britain is included at appendix 2. This includes three nights of accommodation, with meals and tours as specified. The cost of this tour is £395 per person. A tour director is on hand to make all arrangements and to provide information on the places that are being visited. A standard tour to the Lake District includes: • Round-trip Train tickets to Lake District National Park with reserved seats • scenic Lake cruise • visit medieval Hawkshead village • visit to Hill Top (home of Beatrix Potter) • tour through the picturesque Langdale Valleys • visit to Grasmere the inspiration for the English Romantic Poets • Afternoon Tea at the 'World of Beatrix Potter' A standard tour to Liverpoool includes: • Round-trip train tickets to Liverpool with reserved seats • Entry to Beatles Story Exhibition • Time to explore Liverpool • Beatles 'Magical Mystery Tour' including the Cavern Club • Penny Lane and Strawberry Fields
Tailor made	Individuals select their own itinerary with Evan Evans Tours. This could include making their hotel booking in London then booking several day trips out of London as well as some longer tours out of the capital. Evan Evans Tours also has a groups department and they claim: *'We can build a tour programme to suit your group's needs and help you by discussing all aspects of your itinerary. The types of tours that we can offer are endless! If your knowledge of London and the UK is not up to speed, you can rely on one of our team to advise you.'* These tailor made tours vary in cost depending on the number in the party, the length of the tour and the features selected for inclusion in the tour.

131

✓ This provides part evidence for P2 (inbound). I have written fuller notes on the feedback sheet for this task.

Bibliography

Text books

Dale – BTEC National Travel and Tourism (Heinemann, 2007)
   978 0 435 44588 1
Woodhouse et al – BTEC National Travel and Tourism (Hodder Education,
   2007) 978 0 340 94573 5
Various – BTEC National Travel and Tourism (Longman, 2007)
   978 1 405 86807 5

Websites	Brochures from holiday companies
www.eurocamp.co.uk	Eurocamp 2007
www.cosmos.co.uk	Cosmos Summer Sun 2007
www.evanevantours.co.uk	Cosmos Tourama 2007
www.superbreak.com	Superbreak 2007
www.club18-30.com	Club 18–30 Summer 2007 Guide
www.ukinbound.co.uk	
www.aito.co.uk	

Class notes

Appendix 1

Destinations offered by Eurocamp 2007

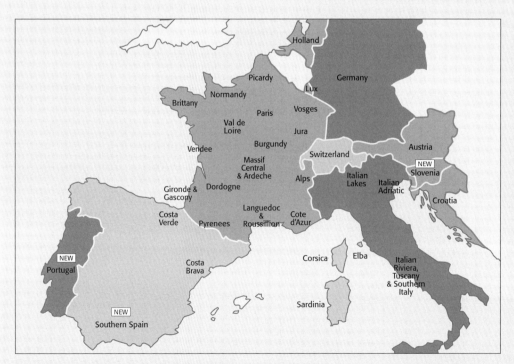

Source: http://www.eurocamp.co.uk/index.cfm?fuseaction=campsites.europeMap&ver=1

Appendix 2

A typical four-day tour offered by Evan Evans Tours:

GEMS OF BRITAIN
Four day tour of Britain.

INCLUDED HIGHLIGHTS

- Tours of Cambridge, York, Edinburgh, Chester and Stratford Upon Avon
- ***Visit Edinburgh Castle and Shakespeare's birthplace***
- 3 nights' accommodation in a first class hotel with 3 breakfasts and 2 dinners

DAY 1 – LONDON – DARLINGTON

We meet our Tour Director this morning and drive north to the university town of Cambridge. Then on to York, where we walk through narrow cobbled streets to the Tudor 'Shambles' and we see York Minster, England's largest medieval cathedral. (D)

DAY 2 – DARLINGTON – EDINBURGH

It's away to Scotland today, across the wild Northumberland Moors and past the romantic ruins of Jedburgh Abbey to Scotland's elegant capital of Edinburgh. (B)

DAY 3 – EDINBURGH – CHESTER

Leaving Edinburgh this morning, we drive through the Southern Uplands. Then it's on to Gretna Green, where many an eloping English couple have been married. Then a delightful drive through the Lake District. (B,D)

DAY 4 – CHESTER – LONDON

This morning we see Chester's unique black and white 'Rows' (shopping arcades) and the town walls which encircle them. Next stop is at the world-famous Wedgwood China factory. Further south, we arrive in Stratford-upon-Avon, where we visit Shakespeare's birthplace. From Stratford we travel along long-established roads through the Cotswolds. Finally we return to London where our memorable tour ends. (B)

(D) = Dinner (B) = Breakfast

Source: http://www.evanevans.co.uk/

ASSESSOR FEEDBACK FORM

Feedback sheet Tour Operator Products and Services Task 1	Achieved
P2 describe the products and services provided by different categories of tour operator	**Categories:** Outbound ✓ Inbound ✓ Domestic ✓ Independent ✓ Specialist ✓ **Product range:** Components of standard package ✓ Tailor made ✓ Range of destinations ✓ Accommodation choices ✓ Transport options ✓ Ancillary products and services ✓ Target markets ✓	Yes

Tutor comments

Well done. This is a well presented and well researched piece of work.

You have shown a good understanding of different categories of tour operators and have provided at least three relevant examples for each of the five required categories.

I liked the table format used for bringing consistency to your descriptions and ensuring that you have covered the required range.

You have included sufficient depth to give the reader a good insight into the product range for each of the selected tour operators, including an overview of the destinations they operate to, types of accommodation and transport options, a typical standard package and clearly identifying their target markets.

You have shown that you are capable of working towards higher grades and I would like to see you stretch yourself a little more by attempting tasks 2 and 3.

Signed: A Teacher   Date: xxxxxx

Student comments

I am pleased with this feedback. I enjoyed researching the different categories of tour operators and finding out about the different types of holidays they offer. I am now going to attempt M2.

Signed: A Student   Date: xxxxxx

MERIT LEVEL ANSWER

Unit 12 – Tour Operations Assignment Task 2

M2 analyse how a selected tour operator's portfolio of products and services meet the needs of its target market(s)

These are the notes that accompany my PowerPoint slides.

Slide 1

Eurocamp Holidays

M2 analyse how a selected tour operator's portfolio of products and services meet the needs of its target market(s)

I am going to analyse how a selected tour operator's portfolio of products and services meets the needs of its target markets. I have decided to base this on Eurocamp.

Slide 2

Eurocamp's Target Markets

- Families
- Couples
- Over 50s

They cater for their needs by:
- having a wide range of accommodation
- using hoiday parks with excellent facilities
- having clubs and activities to meet their needs

Eurocamp's main market is families. Families have differing needs in terms of the budget they have available, the destination e.g. beach or country, facilities for the children e.g. swimming pools, children's clubs, and the type of accommodation.

Eurocamp holidays offer a lot of flexibility which is appealing to families. The way that Eurocamp prices its holidays is also appealing to families because the price that is advertised is the total price for up to six people. This makes it easier for families to budget for their holidays.

Although Eurocamp holidays are based on tent and mobile home accommodation, this is of a very high standard and some of the top of the range mobile homes are luxurious. Tents allow families to enjoy the 'adventure' of camping but without the hassle of having to erect their own tents and take with them a trailer full of equipment. Mobile home accommodation is provided to meet all budgets.

The customer profile is mainly A, B and C1 including families, couples and those over 50. They cater for their needs by:

- having a wide range of accommodation
- using holiday parks with excellent facilities
- having clubs and activities to meet their needs

I am now going to analyse how Eurocamp's portfolio of products and services meets the needs of its target markets and will start by looking at the family market.

Slide 3

The family market

- **Families with babies and toddlers**
- **Families with children aged 4-10**
- **Families with children aged 10+**
- **Families with children aged 13+**

Eurocamp knows that the needs of families change depending on the ages of the children and it offers different products and services for families with children of different ages.

They know that most children like to play with others of a similar age, so the clubs provide activities and entertainment for specific age ranges. One important point is that if a family has two children, one aged 9 and one aged 11 they can go to the same club if they prefer. Although lots of brothers and sisters would like to get away from one another, there are others who would prefer to be together or where parents would feel more comfortable if they were together, so Eurocamp allows them to go to the same club. This can also help if two clubs are running activities at different times so that parents can still relax knowing both children are occupied together.

They divide the families into:

- Families with babies and toddlers
- Families with children aged 4–10
- Families with children aged 10+
- Families with children aged 13+

I am going to describe some of these products and services and analyse how they meet the needs of these different types of families.

Slide 4

Families with babies and toddlers

- 57 toddler-friendly parks
- a range of equipment for toddlers and babies, for example rumble trucks, all-terrain buggies, high chairs, stair gates
- pre-order baby products with www.tinytotsaway.com
- mini fun station and tent
- free holiday insurance for children under 4 years
- Grandparents can go free

Eurocamp has considered that their parks and accommodation must be safe and secure for toddlers and babies and they advertise that they have 57 toddler friendly parks that are situated away from main roads and railways, with no ditches, steep terraces or water hazards and with lots of safe play areas, grass and shade. Parents would feel more relaxed in these surroundings and it would encourage them to book a particular park if it was going to be safer for their children.

It can be hard work packing for a self-drive, self-catering holiday with very young children and Eurocamp has come up with ways of making this easier.

There are various optional products available to help parents travelling with very young children. For example rumble trucks can be hired – these are like pull along carts that you can load up with all your stuff for the beach and toddlers would love to be pulled along in them. Also there are all-terrain buggies that can be pre-booked on selected Toddler Friendly parks. The buggies have large wheels and light handling and are pre-bookable at £3 per day. It is good that parents can pre-book these because you would want to be sure that one would be available so that you can leave your own buggy at home. You can also hire high chairs. Stair gates are provided in mobile homes so that children don't fall down the steps and bed guards are provided in tents and mobile homes so that they don't fall out of bed. Travel cots can also be provided. All of these mean that parents can travel on holiday without having to worry about all of this equipment so Eurocamp is making parents' life easier as well as helping to keep very young children safe.

One very useful service offered in the brochure is to order baby products with tinytotsaway.com. This means that parents can order all of the things they would need on holiday, nappies, baby foods etc and it takes a lot of hassle out of buying in bulk for a holiday and having to pack all of these things. If families are not having to pack the car up with nappies, high chairs, buggies and everything else you need for very young children, this would be a very appealing service and it would mean that the car is much more comfortable as there will be less things to have to find room for.

It can be hard work keeping toddlers busy so Eurocamp has a mini fun station tent that is open for parents to go into and play with their children 7 days a week from 10 am to 7pm.

For parents who want to be able to relax without the children there is also a playgroup for toddlers called Mini Fun Station for toddlers up to aged 4. It is staffed by qualified children's couriers 6 mornings a week. This means parents of young children can have some 'me time' on holiday and that way they can feel as if they have had a break too.

It can be expensive to take children on holiday and to help parents Eurocamp gives free insurance for children under 4 years of age. This will encourage parents to take out Eurocamp's own insurance cover.

If you take a holiday outside of the school holidays, which families with pre-school children can do, grandparents can travel free on some holidays. This would be very appealing to some families as they would have babysitters on tap! However the Eurocamp couriers often offer a babysitting service too.

Slide 5

Families with primary aged children

FunStation 4+

- for children between the age of 4 and 6. Every day there's a different range of fun activities including face painting, dressing up, playing pirates and nature trails.

FunStation 7+

- Daily activities like benchball, uni-hoc, treasure hunts, talent shows and discos
- Some large sites also have soccer clubs
- Junior tents

Primary aged children cannot be left alone and this makes it hectic for parents to keep them occupied all the time. To meet this need Eurocamp has two children's clubs for primary school aged children.

There is Leo's Club for the 4 to 6 year olds. This has specially trained couriers and activities are available every day including things like face painting, dressing up, playing pirates or Leo's nature trail.

The 7 plus club has activities like benchball, uni-hoc, treasure hunts, talent shows and discos as well as giving the children something to do for a few hours, it makes them more independent and they can make new friends.

Some large sites also have soccer clubs.

The clubs are free which means that parents are not having to break into their holiday budget and they would give parents some free time to relax, read a book etc both of which children would find boring. The children might also make some new friends and this can be good, especially for single children. Junior tents can be hired to give children somewhere to play safely.

Slide 6

In between

- *FunStation 10+*
- **The couriers organise team games which is a great way to make new friends**
- **Some activities are organised with Kings Sport Camps, the UK's no.1 provider of multi-activity sports camps and they can also join soccer clubs where available**

Older children (10+) also need to be kept occupied on holiday and many parents find this hard work.

Many children of this age group like team games so this club has lots of activities like basketball, uni-hoc, flag football and orienteering. They can also learn new activities like chinese football. Team games can help children from smaller families have more fun on holiday as they cannot play cricket or other team games properly if they have just their parents on holiday.

Eurocamp has joined up with Kings Sports Camps for some of its activities. This makes sure that activities are well run and safe. They can also join soccer clubs where available

Slide 7

Teenagers

- *Base Club for teenagers*
- The clubs are open for 5 hours a day, 6 days a week
- Sessions are exclusive to teenagers aged 13+

Teenagers have a special base courier who organises get togethers and activities like beach parties and karting.

This can be great for parents because it is difficult to have teenagers on holiday. They often don't like sightseeing or lounging around the pool and most male teenagers hate shopping.

Teenagers like to have a bit of space from their families. If they make friends they can be a lot more independent and the holiday parks are safe for them to go off on their own and meet up with other teenagers.

Slide 8

Single parent families

- 'Arrival Survival' for Single Parent Families
- Discounts for single parent families and members of Gingerbread

Eurocamp helps single parents by offering them help on arrival as it can be hard for a single parent to have to unpack the car on their own while the kids want to get off and explore.

There are also discounts of £65 off the base price for one parent families and members of the club 'Gingerbread' and one parent families can get £100 off a two week holiday, £50 off a 7 night holiday if they travel outside the summer school holidays.

Slide 9

The holiday parks

Holiday parks to meet every need:

- **Large and lively**
- **Small and quiet**
- **Children's playgrounds**
- **Swimming pools**
- **Toddler pools**
- **Slides and flumes**
- **takeaways**

Eurocamp's holiday parks are so varied they have something for everyone.

Families with lively teenagers will be able to choose large and lively parks where there is evening entertainment to keep them occupied. Other small and quiet parks will appeal to families with smaller children. The brochure and website descriptions clearly describe the range of facilities available, including swimming pools, slides, flumes, restaurants, bars, shops and takeaways so that families are very well informed when they make their holiday choices.

Slide 10

Children's representatives

Eurocamp Children's Representatives must:
- Hold a NNEB or NVQ in Childcare or equivelent
- Have at least 6 months-1 year experience working with children
- Have a valid First Aid Certificate

Their main responsibilities are:
- Organising daytime and evening activities
- Supervising early suppers
- Telling bedtime stories
- Focusing on the health and safety of the children

Parents want to know that their children are safe on holiday and that the representatives are well qualified and trained. Eurocamp representatives have to have a relevant childcare qualification, experience of working with children and a First aid qualification.

They can meet parents' needs by organising daytime and evening activities, supervising early suppers, telling bedtime stories, focusing on the health and safety of the children

Slide 11

Other target markets
- Over 50s
- Couples
- Fishing
- Activity eg cycling, canoeing
- Walking and wildlife
- Cultural
- City breaks e.g. Paris, Venice, Rome
- Flight options

143

Most Eurocamp holidays are offered from May until September and they need to try and keep their accommodation as full as possible for the whole season. They have no problem filling up during the main school holidays but they still need to sell the 'shoulder' seasons and they target couples and over 50s to do this.

Many couples and over 50s take several holidays a year and these would be appealing to them. The prices are so much cheaper to encourage people to book at these times. Also Eurocamp has 'themed' some of its holiday parks to appeal to these markets including fishing, activity holidays such as cycling and canoeing, walking and wildlife, cultural and city breaks, including parks convenient for Paris, Venice and Rome. The family sized accommodation is very spacious for couples and the parks are quite quiet outside school holidays so older people can get a flexible and very reasonably priced holiday in lovely areas in Europe. Flight options and car hire are also available for those on a tighter schedule.

Slide 12

Conclusion

Eurocamp has an excellent portfolio of products and services to meet the needs of families

Out of season their products and services also provide excellent value for money holidays for couples and over 50s.

This presentation shows that Eurocamp is constantly adapting its products and services to meet the needs of its target groups and that it has a particularly good understanding of what is needed by the family markets and especially for children of different ages. The portfolio of products and services is extensive for the family market and will help the children AND their parents get more out of their holiday. They also offer excellent value for money holidays for couples and over 50s out of season and are adapting a range of special interest holidays to meet their needs.

ASSESSOR FEEDBACK FORM

Feedback sheet Tour Operator Products and Services Task 2		Achieved
M2 analyse how a selected tour operator's portfolio of products and services meet the needs of its target market(s)	**Evidence:** PowerPoint slides and notes Observation record	Yes

Tutor comments

A good presentation, well supported by PowerPoint slides and notes.

Please refer to separate observation record.

Signed: A Teacher   Date: xxxxxx

Student comments

I did not realise that holiday companies add so many extra things to cater for different markets.

I enjoyed researching Eurocamp because I can see how it would meet the needs of my own family.

Signed: A Student   Date: xxxxxx

OBSERVATION RECORD

Student name:	A STUDENT
Programme name	**BTEC National Certificate in Travel and Tourism**
Unit:	**12: Tour Operations**
Which parts of the unit have been met? M2	**Observation notes: How the student's performance met the requirements of the specification** This was a good presentation. You have carried out detailed research into the company and its products and services and have reviewed these systematically in the context of the target market, with particular reference to the family market. Within your presentation you have analysed how the products and services meet the needs of the family market. Well done for acknowledging the different needs within this market and showing how Eurocamp has adapted to meet these needs. You have equally recognised the need for Eurocamp to target different markets at different times of the year and have shown how the products and services can also meet the needs of couples and over 50s. Your presentation was delivered knowledgably and with some confidence. You made eye contact with your audience although you were a little reliant on your notes in places. With practice you should be able to further develop your presentation skills. Well done!

How, when and where the activity took place?

PowerPoint presentation, observed by tutor and class. Room 6 on xxxx date at xxxx time.

Observer's name: A TEACHER

Observer's signature: A Teacher   Date: xxxxx

Student signature: A Student   Date: xxxxx

DISTINCTION LEVEL ANSWER

Unit 12 – Tour Operations Assignment Task 3

D2 recommend, with justification, how a selected tour operator could expand its range of products and services for its current target market or adapt its range of products and services to appeal to a new market

Eurocamp is constantly revamping and improving its products and services and it is difficult to see where improvements can be made or where it could expand.

The recommendations that I am going to make are:

1. to develop activity holidays with PGL

2. to launch a winter activity programme

3. to develop eco-friendly accommodation

To develop activity holidays with PGL

If I was travelling with my family on a Eurocamp holiday I would not be particularly keen on going to the Children's Club. Although the activities sound good it doesn't really sound cool to be going to the Base club.

In 2007 PGL was bought by Holidaybreak so it is part of the same company as Eurocamp (see appendix 1).

I think this is one area where Eurocamp could expand. PGL offer most of their overseas holidays to school groups, which means travelling mainly during term time. This will mean that their activity centres and staff are less busy during the school holidays and this is when Eurocamp is most busy.

I would recommend that Eurocamp starts to offer PGL packages to families staying near to their activity centres. PGL owns 7 sites and Eurocamp could look to see if any of these are of a good enough standard for their market and then contract to put their own accommodation onto these parks. This would mean that families could have the quality of Eurocamp accommodation and all the extras they provide, while combining this with great PGL activities for the children. The courses would last only 5 days so families would still get to have time together but parents would be able to go off and do sightseeing etc knowing that their children were having a brilliant time.

PGL does offer some family holidays during the summer but they are for the whole family to take part in activities, whereas parents might prefer to do other things like shopping and sightseeing which they would be able to do on Eurocamp Holidays. I believe this would give families the best of both worlds and it could attract families who have children who like adventure sports and activities and who might not previously have considered taking a Eurocamp holiday. There is the added bonus that PGL is recognised as a reputable company in its own right and this would give parents more peace of mind than booking adventure activities with an unknown overseas organiser.

Winter Activity programmes

The Eurocamp season is very short, usually running from May until September. This means that their mobile homes are out of action for 7 months of the year. It also means that their staff work for quite short seasons.

Eurocamp uses a number of holiday parks in Alpine areas. Mobile homes are well equipped nowadays for year round use and I believe Eurocamp should consider featuring a number of winter holidays in these areas. Some of the competition, for example Al Fresco, already do this, but Eurocamp is better known and should try and get into this market.

They could offer self drive or flight programmes (just as they do in the summer), for example flying to Geneva and then using resorts in the French Alps. I believe these holidays would appeal to its current family market as it would make winter sport holidays more affordable. They should choose resorts where there are a range of activities to suit different members of the family.

Eco-friendly accommodation

Green tourism is becoming 'big business' and lots of holiday companies are keen to advertise that they are environmentally friendly. Eurocamp is a reputable independent company selling 'outdoor' holidays and they should be one of the leaders in promoting environmentally friendly holidays. Eurocamp already encourages holidaymakers to recycle and not waste water but more and more people are attracted by 'green tourism'.

Eurocamp has recently started to introduce chalets into their programmes and I would recommend that they look at developing this with special 'eco friendly' chalets on holiday parks where the chalets can be placed in more natural environments, like in woodland. Bicycles should be available for hire and walks, bike rides and other activities could be organised to fit in with the natural theme. If the cost of introducing chalets is too great then maybe specially adapted environmentally friendly mobile homes should be introduced.

The chalets should use solar energy and be fitted with energy efficient equipment. Natural products should be used where possible. The parks themselves would have excellent recycling facilities.

Just as Eurocamp advertise their toddler friendly parks, they could advertise these 'eco-friendly' parks. Many people take their responsibilities to the environment very seriously and I believe this initiative would appeal to both current market and attract new customers.

Task 3 Appendix 1

From The Times
May 19, 2007

PGL bagged by Holidaybreak for £100m

DOMINIC WALSH

Management at Britain's biggest school and activity holiday operator will share almost £50 million after agreeing a sale of the business to Holidaybreak for £100 million.

PGL, known affectionately as Parents Get Lost, is being sold for more than double the £42 million paid less than two years ago by management with backing from Royal Bank of Scotland when the late founder's family was bought out.

The bank, which supplied the debt funding in the 2005 deal, will receive about £2 million for its 4 per cent stake. But the biggest beneficiary will be Martin Davies, PGL's chief executive, who is expected to receive almost £10 million.

Mr Davies and his colleagues will remain with the business, which will become Holidaybreak's fourth division, alongside hotel breaks, adventure travel and camping. He will join the board as divisional managing director.

PGL, which will remain based in Ross-on-Wye, was founded in 1957 by Peter Gordon Lawrence. Mr Lawrence started the venture with canoe camping trips for groups of teenagers on the River Wye.

Today, PGL sends more than 250,000 children to its own network of 26 activity centres or on overseas tours and skiing holidays. It has 17 sites in Britain, eight in France and one in Spain and last year made an operating profit of £6.3 million on turnover of £50.6 million.

Carl Michel, Holidaybreak's chief executive, said that he intended to expand the business both organically and through acquisition: "PGL ticks all our strategic boxes and will make an excellent fourth leg."

He said that he would continue to look at further small acquisitions in other areas, particularly for Holidaybreak's adventure travel division. "We have a healthy pipeline of deal opportunities. Watch this space," Mr Michel said.

The group announced the deal alongside half-year results, which showed its normal seasonal losses before tax widening from £6.3 million to £7.9 million. Revenue increased from £88.7 million to £100.6 million and the interim dividend is up 10 per cent at 8.8p.

Mr Michel said that, despite a difficult market, current trading was in line with expectations, with sales from hotel breaks up 8 per cent thanks to popular theatres shows in London.

Sales from its camping arm, which Holidaybreak tried to sell last year, are flat on capacity down 4 per cent and Mr Michel said that he saw no reason to make a fresh attempt to sell it given its strong cash generation. "Nothing is ever permanent but it's a cash cow and produces strong returns."

http://business.timesonline.co.uk/tol/business/industry_sectors/leisure/article1810997.ece

ASSESSOR FEEDBACK FORM

Feedback sheet Tour Operator Products and Services Task 3		Achieved
D2 recommend, with justification, how a selected tour operator could expand its range of products and services for its current target market or adapt its range of products and services to appeal to a new market	Recommendations ✓ Justification ✓	 Yes

Tutor comments

Well done, you have made some interesting recommendations and given some justification for your choices.

Your recommendations would enable Eurocamp to extend its appeal to its current markets as well as targeting new customers.

Signed: A Teacher   Date: xxxxxx

Student comments

I am very pleased with this as I am aiming for a distinction as a final grade in this unit.

Signed: A Student   Date: xxxxxx